THE OFFICIAL EXPLANATIONS

D0124149

Books by Paul Dickson

Think Tanks

The Great American Ice Cream Book

The Future of the Workplace

The Electronic Battlefield

The Mature Person's Guide to Kites, Yo-Yos, Frisbees and Other
Childlike Diversions

Out of This World: American Space Photography

The Future File

Chow: A Cook's Tour of Military Food

The Official Rules

The Official Explanations

Paul Dickson

THE OFFICIAL EXPLANATIONS

Illustrated by Kenneth Tiews

DELACORTE PRESS/NEW YORK

Published by
Delacorte Press
1 Dag Hammarskjold Plaza
New York, N.Y. 10017

Manufactured in the United States of America

First printing

Designed by Giorgetta Bell McRee

Library of Congress Cataloging in Publication Data

Dickson, Paul.
The official explanations.

Includes index.
1. American wit and humor.   I. Title.
PN6162.D48   081   80–11373

ISBN 0–440–06513–5

PN
6162
.D48

ACKNOWLEDGMENTS

Excerpts from "This Way to the Exit" by Dr. Ross K. Baker: © 1978 by The New York Times Company. Reprinted by permission.

"Children's Birthday Parties" and "Adults at Parties" from *MY WAR WITH THE 20TH CENTURY* by Pierre Berton: Copyright © 1965 by Pierre Berton. Reprinted by permission of Doubleday & Company, Inc., and Curtis Brown, Ltd.

"Gerrold's Law" and "Short's Quotations": copyright © 1980 by David Gerrold. Used by permission.

Excerpt from "Getting In On A Zurich" by Dan Jenkins: reprinted courtesy of *Sports Illustrated,* September 4, 1978. © 1978 Time Inc.

"Murphy's Marketing Maxims": © 1971, Schoonmaker Associates, P.O. Drawer M, Coram, N.Y. 11727.

"Murray's Laws": Copyright © 1978, *Los Angeles Times.* Reprinted with permission.

"Robert's Rules of Home and Garden": Reprinted with permission from the *Chicago Sun-Times.* Excerpts from the column "Poor Robert's Almanac for Home Handymen and Gardeners" by Bob Herguth.

"Rosenblatt's Rules": Copyright © 1979 *The Washington Post.*

Time "Letters" column, March 19, 1979, for Boettcher's Attribution, Close's Law, Coccia's Law, and Ogden's Law: Copyright 1979 Time Inc. All rights reserved.

To The Fellows of
the Murphy Center

The Murphy Guide to the Special Sections

Preface

"Never try to be nice to man with a tattoo on his face" was all that one note said. Yet another envelope in the same day's mail contained no fewer than 150 laws, maxims, injunctions, and explanations. This is the range of the material coming to the attention of the nation's smallest and least organized think tank, the revered Murphy Center for the Codification of Human and Organizational Law.

Founded in 1976 and housed in a small oak file-box, the Center has become an important international clearinghouse for concise discoveries about the world and how it *really* operates. In 1978 the Center published its first research report in book form, titled *The Official Rules.* That publication brought the work of the Center to the attention of many people who have been in touch with its Director to share their own universal discoveries.

To date the Center has collected some 5,000 rules, laws, principles, maxims, and "whatevers," with more coming in each day. Two annexes have been added to the original site (a pair of cardboard file-boxes), the Center's existence has been noted by the national news media, and the names of hundreds of dedicated contributors have been added to the roll of the Official Fellows of the Center. This title is bestowed on people who contribute to the work of the Center in accord with *The Compensation Corollary,* which states, "In a society where credentials are important, the cheapest form of payment is a fancy title." This is closely associated with *The Resume Rule:* "With few exceptions (Jack the Ripper, Attila the Hun, etc.) just about anyone can be made to look good on a piece of paper."

If the submissions coming into the Center are a barometer for our collective state of mind at this point in history, it would seem that we are doing pretty well despite OPEC, Congress, rampant automation, inflation, the energy crisis, and the many other ducks that collectively threaten to peck us to death. Specifically, the material is comfortably cynical, puckish, unswayed by large institutions, and possessed of a widespread quasi-religious faith in gremlins, institutional tomfoolery, human imperfectibility, and the perversity of inanimate objects.

The majority of the submissions to the Center are original, homespun, grassroots; products of the fertile mind of the contributor, but a number are statements originated by other, often famous, individuals. For what it may be worth to aspiring sociologists, the Center has experienced a run on statements originally made by Calvin Coolidge and Samuel Goldwyn. Examples:

Goldwyn on Thinking Small: Why only twelve disciples? Go out and get thousands.

Coolidge on Compensation: Thank you. Come again. (To the Treasury official who brought him his first salary check as President.)

What follows is a healthy selection of the best of what is coming into the Center, with additional material gleaned from the Director's own research. A large number of good items that have been sent to the Center do not appear for reasons of space or because of their unintentional similarity to other items. So, too, a number have been excluded because they violate the good-taste standards of an august and venerable research institute. (For instance, a law named for a recent President of the United States, which was rejected, stated, "When the going gets tough, the tough get phlebitis.")

The report is arranged alphabetically, with a number of special sections worked in among the individual items. These special sections cover areas that especially interest the Center. To the extent possible the person who discovered the law or rule and its source are identified. To save valuable space some sources that appear frequently have been abbreviated. They can be deciphered with the aid of the "Source Code" that appears at the back of the book, just ahead of the listing of Fellows and the news- and gossip-laden first issue of *The Center Newsletter,* which appears without cost or obligation (no salesman will call).

Meanwhile, the Center will continue to collect and sort immutable truths for future reports of this nature, and it welcomes correspondence (as well as large open-ended, no-strings financial grants) at the address below.

Finally, should anyone wonder about the title of this report, you can find the source of inspiration on page 168, under the heading "Official Explanations, Law of."

Paul Dickson, Director
The Murphy Center
Box 80
Garrett Park, MD 20766

THE OFFICIAL EXPLANATIONS

- **Abercrombie's Theory of Parallel Universes.** There exists a parallel universe into which all our lost objects are sucked, never to be seen again.

    (Denis Abercrombie, from Larry Groebe.)

- **Abourezk's First Eight Laws of Politics.** (1) Anybody who really would change things for the better in this country could never be elected president anyway. (2) Don't worry about your enemies, it's your allies who will do you in. (3) In politics people will do whatever is necessary to get their way. (4) The bigger the appropriations bill, the shorter the debate. (5) If a politician has a choice between listening and talking, guess which one he will choose. (6) When voting on the confirmation of a presidential appointment, it's always safer to vote against the son of a bitch, because if he is confirmed, it won't be long before he proves how wise you were. (7) If you want to curry favor with a politician, give him credit for something that someone else did. (8) Don't blame me, I voted for McGovern.

    (Senator James Abourezk, from his article "Life Inside the Congressional Cookie Jar," *Playboy,* March 1979.)

- **Acheson's Comment on Experts.** An expert is like a eunuch in a harem—someone who knows all about it but can't do anything about it.

    (Dean Acheson. *TCA.*)

- **Ackley's Axiom.** The degree of technical competence is inversely proportional to the level of management.

    (Bob Ackley, T.Sgt., USAF, Plattsmouth, Neb. He adds,

"Originally defined—in 1967—as 'The level of intelligence is inversely proportional to the number of stripes,' then I had to modify it as I accrued more stripes.")

● **Adams's Axiom.** It doesn't matter what you say, as long as you keep talking.
(Harold "Buck" Adams, Capt., USAF, c. 1974, from Bob Ackley, Plattsmouth, Neb.)

● **Adams's Law of Gossip.** Ninety-two percent of the stuff told you in confidence you couldn't get anyone else to listen to.
(Journalist, poet, and humorist Franklin Pierce Adams.)

● **Adams's Political Discovery.** Practical politics consists in ignoring facts.
(Historian Henry Adams.)

● **Ade's Reminder.** A bird in the hand may be worth two in the bush, but remember also that a bird in the hand is a positive embarrassment to one not in the poultry business.
(Humorist George Ade.)

● **Adenauer's Advice.** An infallible method of conciliating a tiger is to allow oneself to be devoured.
(Dr. Konrad Adenauer.)

● **Adlai's Axiom.** He who slings mud generally loses ground.
(Adlai Stevenson, 1954. *MLS.*)

● **Agrait's Law.** A rumor will travel fastest to the place where it will cause the greatest harm.
(Gustavo N. Agrait, Rio Piedras, P. R.)

● **"Ain't": Why Americans Say It.** (1) Because there ain't no reason not to. (2) Because there ain't no easy way to prove there're not reasons to. (3) Because at times it serves the purpose in communicating.

> (Editor Lucy Catherine Bowie, in the *Madison County* [Va.] *Eagle* when she learned that the government was about to issue a grant of $121,000 to find out why many Americans say "ain't.")

● **Air Force Law.** Two percent don't get the word.
(U/GT.)

● **Albert's Law of the Sea.** The more they are in a fog, the more boats (and people) toot their horns.

> (Bernard L. Albert, M.D., Scarsdale, N.Y.)

● **Albinak's Algorithm.** When graphing a function, the width of the line should be inversely proportional to the precision of the data.

> (Marvin J. Albinak, Professor of Chemistry, Essex Community College, Baltimore, Md.)

AIR FORCE LAW

● **Alderson's Theorem.** If at first you don't succeed, you are running about average.

    (M. H. Alderson, from the *Lawrence County* [Mo.] *Record.*)

● **Alfalfa's Observation.** Another day, another zero!
(From T. A. Moore III, M.D., New Orleans, who recalls it from "a memorable scene in the Our Gang comedies when Spanky, Buckwheat, and Alfalfa are descending the steps of their school after another day of intellectual disaster." Moore adds, "This is certainly a universal sentiment and could not be more succinct.")

● **Alicat Shop Generalization.** The more gushing they do, the less they buy.

    (Florenz Baron, Yonkers, N.Y. Named for the Alicat Bookshop run by Florenz and her late husband, Oscar.)

● **Alice's Law.** The purpose of Presidential office is not power, or leadership of the Western World, but reminiscence, best-selling reminiscence.

    (Roger Jellinek, *The New York Times Book Review,* March 10, 1968.)

● **Allan's Theorem.** In any group of eagles, you will find some turkeys.

    (Allan B. Guerrina, Woodbridge, Va.)

● **Allen's Circus Axiom.** If a circus is half as good as it smells, it's a great show.

    (Radio with Fred Allen.)

● **Allen's Motto.** I'd rather have a free bottle in front of me than a prefrontal lobotomy.

    (Fred Allen. *DRW.*)

● **Anderson's Maxims.** (1) Colleges and universities are immune to their own knowledge. (2) You can't outthink a person who isn't thinking.

> (Phil Anderson, Assistant Professor, College of St. Thomas, St. Paul, Minn.)

● **Anderson's Observation.** Institutions tend to treat their employees as they do their clients. Schools, prisons, uptight corporations, etc., structure time for their clients and employees as well. Laid-back free clinics, certain mental health units, universities, etc., do not structure time for their clients; thus they do not structure time for their employees.

> (E. Frederick Anderson, Assistant Dean, San Diego State University.)

● **Anonymous's Bodily Discovery.** Whatever doesn't stick out is hanging down.

> (Name withheld by request.)

● **Apartment Dweller's Law.** One person's floor is another person's ceiling.

> *(U/Ra.)*

● **Aquinas Axiom, The.** What the gods get away with, the cows don't.

> *(DRW.)*

● **Armor's Axiom of Morality.** Virtue is the failure to achieve vice.

> (John C. Armor, Baltimore.)

● **Arnofy's Law of the Post Office.** The likelihood of a letter getting lost in the mail is directly proportional to its importance.

(Andrew G. Aronfy, M.D., Seabrook, Md. Aronfy's proof: "I sent the IRS a substantial check for estate taxes. A month and a half later they sent us a bill for an additional $207.00 for interest and penalties. Needless to say, they never got the original.")

● **Arnold's Square Wheel Theory.** A prevalent form of decision-making holds that if three out of four schools, firms, or whatever, are using square wheels then the fourth will follow.
(Richard Arnold, Keezletown, Va.)

● **Astor's Economic Discovery.** A man who has a million dollars is as well off as if he were rich.
(John Jacob Astor.)

● **Augustine's Plea.** Give me chastity and self-restraint, but do not give it yet.
(Saint Augustine.)

● **Aunt Emmie's Laws.** (1) A cigarette placed in an ashtray will go out if you stay in the room; if you leave the room, the cigarette will topple to the table, burn through, and drop to the floor, where it will smolder until it descends to ignite the drapes in the room below. (2) A clever remark is one you don't make at the appropriate moment but compose immediately after. (3) A pair of scissors should be a true pair; the second pair is to be used in place of the pair that is never where it is always supposed to be.
(Owen Elliott, Ridgefield, Conn. Aunt Emmie was the youngest of his mother's eight sisters.)

● **Austin's Law.** It tastes better in somebody else's house.
(Mabel Austin, New York City. Submitted by Mrs. Mariquita P. Mullan.)

B

● **Baber's Rule.** Anything worth doing is worth doing in excess.
(Susan Baber, St. Louis.)

● **Bacchanalian Conclusion.** One can get just as drunk on water . . . as one can on land!
(Eldred O. Schwab, Ojibwa, Wisc.)

● **Backus's Law.** All water is one inch over your boot tops. (Named for Dr. Richard Backus of Woods Hole and reported by Ken S. Norris, Professor of Natural History, Santa Cruz, Cal. Norris, who says, "No law I know is more completely immutable," adds that he and Backus have sighted a rock south of Cape Horn that offers a silhouette close to that of Backus with water sloshing over his boots.)

● **Bair's Rule of Lighting.** Fuses never blow during daylight hours. *Corollary:* Only after the fuses blow do you discover the flashlight batteries are dead and you're out of candles, or matches, or both.
(Penny Bair, Austin, Tex.)

● **Baker's Byroad.** When you are over the hill, you pick up speed.
(U/DRW.)

● **Baker's Secrets of Losing Politics.** (1) Address yourself to the issues. (2) Identify as closely as possible with politicians.

(3) Be a loyal party person. (4) Invoke the memories of your party greats. (5) If you are squeamish about your partisanship, at least have the good grace to refer to the accomplishments of your party's major officeholders. (6) Take the high road. (7) Never criticize your opponent's absenteeism on votes if you are seeking his congressional seat. (8) Never criticize your opponent for spending too much time in the district. (9) Avoid squandering huge amounts of money in media markets where only a fraction of the television audience is made up of your potential voters. (10) Forget about the endorsements of Hollywood celebrities and sports figures.

> (Ross K. Baker, Professor of Political Science, Rutgers University. First revealed in *The New York Times,* December 5, 1978.)

● **Ballweg's Discovery.** Whenever there is a flat surface, someone will find something to put on it.

> (Col. Lawrence H. Ballweg, USAF [retired], Albuquerque, N.M.)

● **Balzer's Law.** Life is what happens to you while you are making other plans.

> (Robert Balzer.)

● **Banacek's Law.** When the owl shows up at the mouse picnic, he's not there to enter the sack race.

> (TV character "Banacek" [George Peppard]. *MLS.*)

● **Barber's Rule of Uniformity.** If it sticks out, cut it off.
> (Linda Marsh, barber, Portland, Ore., from Gary M. Knowlton.)

● **Barilleaux's Observations on Eating Out.** (1) The price of the meal varies directly with the accent of the waiter. (2) If you need help to translate the menu, you can't afford the meal. (3)

If a salad is served with the meal, the portions will be smaller. (4) If soup is also served with the meal, the portions will be even smaller.

(Ryan J. Barilleaux, Lafayette, La.)

● **Barnes's Law of Probability.** There's a 50 percent chance of anything—either it happens or it doesn't.

(Michael R. Barnes, Dallas. *JS.*)

● **Barnum's Dictum.** Every crowd has a silver lining.

(P. T. Barnum.)

● **Baron's Law.** The world is divided between victims and predators, and you have to defend yourself against both.

(Florenz Baron, Yonkers, N.Y.)

● **Barrymore's Conclusion.** The thing that takes up the least amount of time and causes the most amount of trouble is Sex.

(John Barrymore.)

● **Bartel's Law.** When someone is kicking your ass, at least you know when you are out in front.

(Donald E. Bartel, Palo Alto, Cal.)

● **Bartlett's Observation of Input/Output.** The problem with pulling names out of a hat is that it is possible that you'll end up with a size.

(H. A. Bartlett, East Norwalk, Conn.)

● **Battista's Explanation.** The fellow who says he'll meet you halfway usually thinks he's standing on the dividing line.

(O. A. Battista, *The Philadelphia Bulletin.*)

● **Bax's Rule.** You should make a point of trying every experience once—except incest and folk dancing.

    (Arnold Bax, quoted by Nigel Rees in *Quote . . . Unquote,* George Allen and Unwin, 1978.)

● **Beckmann's Lemma.** Where there is no patrol car, there is no speed limit.

    (Petr Beckmann, from Richard Stone, Stanford, Cal., who insists his friend's name is actually spelled Petr.)

● **Bedard's Laws of Fossil Fuel.** (1) The last gas station for 50 miles will be closed when you get there. (2) At the moment of any departure, the level of gas in your tank depends entirely on how late you are. (3) You only run out of gas after your wife tells you to stop for gas before you run out.

    (Patrick Bedard, *Car and Driver* magazine.)

● **Beebe's Law for Teachers and Preachers.** Heads should be weighed, not counted.

    (Rev. Richard K. Beebe, Litchfield, Conn.)

● **Beiser's Brass Tack.** Facts without theory is trivia. Theory without facts is bullshit.

    (U/RA.)

● **Belknap's Fat Flow Formula.** Fat is lost where it is wanted the least. *Corollary 1:* Fat is lost first from areas of high desirability. *Corollary 2:* With time fat flows from areas of high to low desirability.

    (Hal R. Belknap, M.D., Norman, Okla.)

● **Bell's Law of Frustration.** When responding to an urgent message requesting an immediate return call, you will get: (1) a wrong number, (2) a busy signal, or (3) no answer.

    (Named for Ma and Alexander Graham Bell by Joseph P. Sullivan, Indianapolis.)

● **Bell's Rules.** (1) The average time between throwing something away and needing it badly is two weeks. This time can be reduced to one week by retaining the thing for a long time first. (2) Linear objects (such as wire, string, etc.), when left to their own devices, occupy time by twisting themselves into tangles and weaving knots. (3) Tiny objects, when dropped, run and hide. (4) There is an updraft over wastebaskets.

(Norman R. Bell, Associate Professor of Engineering, North Carolina State University.)

● **Benchley's Travel Distinction.** In America there are two classes of travel—first class, and with children.

(Robert Benchley.)

● **Bendiner's Election Rule.** No matter how frighteningly the campaigners warn you that the salvation of the world depends on their winning, remember that on November 9, half of them will be wiring congratulations to the other half on their great victory and promising to co-operate fully in the predicted disaster.

(Robert Bendiner, from his article "How to Listen to Campaign Oratory If You Have To," *Look,* October 11, 1960.)

● **Bennett's Accidental Discoveries.** (1) Most auto accidents are caused by people with driver's licenses, so I tore up my license. (2) According to the latest statistics most auto accidents happen within 8 miles of your own home, so I moved.

(William S. Bennett, San Mateo, Cal.)

● **Berg's Constant.** Every time you learn a new word, you hear it five times the next day.

(Stephanie Berg, *Johns Hopkins Magazine,* May 1978.)

BENCHLEY'S TRAVEL DISTINCTION

● **Berger's Economics for the Masses.** The more there are of anything, the less they cost. Exclusivity has its price.
(Martin Berger, Mount Vernon, N.Y.)

● **Berkeley Beatitude.** The real world is just a special case of the theoretical.
(Don Smith, MBA, University of California Berkeley.)

● **Berliner's Law of Mineral Propagation.** Wire coat hangers multiply in dark closets.
(The late Josephine Mitchell Berliner, Washington, D.C., from her daughter Joie Vargas, Reno, Nev.)

● **Bernstein's Book Principles.**
Set I. Acquisition by Purchase. (1) If you buy a hardcover edition of a book, the paperback edition will appear next week, at a much lower price. (2) If you buy a paperback edition of a book, the hardcover will be remaindered next week, at a much lower price. (3) If you buy a paperback edition, or a hardcover edition, or a remaindered copy of a book, the next week you will find that a copy in excellent condition will be available in a used-book shop—at a much lower price than any of the other three. (4) If you buy a used hardcover copy of a book, a new edition that will make all previous editions obsolete will appear in hardcover next week. (5) A publisher will allow a book to go out of print just in time for you to begin looking for it. . . .
Set II. Borrowing from a Library. (1) If you go to the library for a book, the library will probably not have it in its collection. (2) If it does have the book in its collection, it will be checked out, or overdue, or lost, or stolen. (3) If it does have the book at hand, the pages you need to consult will be torn out. (4) If the book is available, at hand, and undamaged, it will probably be outdated and therefore useless. (5) If the book is available, at hand, un-damaged, and current, it will probably be too useful to be

used effectively in the library away from your other materials, and it will not be in the circulating collection. . . .

(Richard B. Bernstein, *Harvard Law Record,* Cambridge, Mass. From his larger collection of Book Principles.)

● **Bernstein's Law of Declining Progress.** One begins to lose interest in any given task and slacks off just as one is beginning to get somewhere in accomplishing that task.

(Richard B. Bernstein again.)

● **Berra's Rule of Attendance.** If the people don't want to come out, there's no way you're gonna stop 'em.

(Yogi Berra, from Steven D. Mirsky, Ithaca, N.Y.)

● **Beshere's Formula for Failure.** There are only two kinds of people who fail: those who listen to nobody, and . . . those who listen to everybody.

(Thomas M. Beshere, Jr., Charleston, S.C.)

● **Bethell's Iron Law of Washington.** The laws of supply and demand do not apply to Washington, they are turned inside out. Problems elsewhere in the country merely contribute to the wealth of Washington.

(Tom Bethell in *Harper's* magazine.)

● **Bialac's Conclusion.** Statistics are no substitute for common sense.

(Richard N. Bialac, Cincinnati, Ohio.)

● **Big Mac Principle, The.** The whole is equal to more than the sum of its parts. The whole is equal to less than the sum of its parts.

(Robert J. Samuelson, *The National Journal,* August 12, 1978. This apparently contradictory Principle bears some explanation. In Samuelson's own words, "Anyone can understand the relationship of these truths to the real-life Big Mac. A Big Mac, of course, is 'two all-beef patties, special sauce, lettuce, cheese, pickles, onion on a sesame seed bun.' Depending on your taste, these few ingredients produce one of the magnificent gastronomical delights of American civilization *[the whole is equal to more than the sum of its parts]* or an insult to the sensitive stomach *[the whole is equal to less than the sum of its parts].*" He says that the Principle explains a lot about what is going on in Washington as things fall on one side or the other of the more-than/less-than scale. It explains, for instance, why as Congress becomes harder working and better educated, it falls in public esteem and contributes to the general creakiness of government. Congress then is equal to less than the sum of its parts.)

● **Bilbo's Proverb.** Never laugh at live dragons. *(U/GT.)*

● **Billings's Advice (a smattering).** (1) Don't ever prophesy; for if you prophesy wrong, nobody will forget it; and if you prophesy right, nobody will remember it. (2) Never work before breakfast; if you have to work before breakfast, get your breakfast first. (3) There are two things in this life for which we are never fully prepared and that is—twins. (4) I don't care how much a man talks, if he only says it in a few words.
(American humorist Josh Billings, 1818–85.)

● **Bing's Rule of Oblique Logic.** Don't try to stem the tide; move the beach.
(Wallace Bing, Mill Valley, Cal.)

● **Bishop's Theorem.** When you have accumulated sufficient knowledge to get by, you're too old to remember it.
(Columnist Jim Bishop.)

● **Bismarck's Laws.** (1) The less people know about how sausages and laws are made, the better they'll sleep at night. (2) When you say that you agree to a thing in principle, you mean that you have not the slightest intention of carrying it out in practice.

(Bismarck.)

● **Bixby's Law of Theater Seating.** In any given row the people with seats on the aisle always arrive first. *Corollary:* The probability that someone in the middle of the row will leave during the performance is directly proportional to the number of persons to be climbed over in reaching the aisle.

(Sandra W. Bixby, Chicago.)

● **Blattenberger's Marital Principle.** Marriages are like union contracts in that six weeks after the fact, both parties feel that they could have done better if they had held out a little longer.

(Larry A. Blattenberger, Martinsburg, Penn.)

● **Blewett's Rules for Dealing with Difficult Personalities.** (1) Identify the bears. (2) Tree the bears. (3) Stroke the bears. (4) Never forget how many bears you've treed. (5) Never let on to the bears who the other bears are. For that matter, never let any of the other creatures in the forest know who the bears are.

(Lt. Col. John H. Blewett, U.S. Army.)

● **Blick's Rule of Life.** You have two chances, slim and none.

(*U*/ From J. Patricia Reilly, New York City.)

● **Blumenthal's Observation on Government.** The difference between business and government is that the government has no bottom line.

(Secretary of the Treasury W. Michael Blumenthal. *TCA.*)

● **Bobbitt's Law of TV.** Television network trouble never occurs except during the most exciting part of your favorite TV show.

    (Larry D. Bobbitt, Amarillo, Tex.)

● **Boettcher's Attribution.** If you have a bunch of clowns, you're going to have a circus.

    (R. J. Boettcher, Bridgewater, N.J. Letters to the Editor, *Time*, March 19, 1979. Boettcher attributes the maxim to the late W. L. Gilman.)

● **Bone's Labor Discovery.** Unlimited manpower can solve any problem except what to do with the manpower; e.g. if a man can dig a hole in a minute, why can't sixty men dig a hole in one second?

    (Jonathan Bone, Chicago.)

● **Boorstin's Observation.** Two centuries ago, when a great man appeared, people looked for God's purpose in him; today we look for his press agent.

    (Daniel J. Boorstin, from *The Image, or, What Happened to the American Dream,* Atheneum.)

● **Borklund's Law.** Communications is equal to the square root of the mistakes times confusion times contradictions.

    (C. W. Borklund, from a November 1966 editorial in *Armed Forces Management* magazine.)

● **Boroson's Conclusion.** There is always a professor of astronomy at a major Ivy League university who believes that the world is flat.

    (Warren Boroson.)

● **Borstelmann's Rule.** If everything seems to be coming your way, you're probably in the wrong lane.

    (U/DRW.)

● **Boucher's Corollary to Murphy's Law.** Murphy's Law holds no more than 80 percent of the time; unfortunately, it is impossible to predict when.

(Wayne Boucher, from his article "A Practical Guide for Perplexed Managers," *MBA Magazine,* August/September 1978.)

● **Boyd's Criteria for Good County Fairs.** (1) A really good fair must have enormous traffic jams and lousy parking. (2) Good carnivals must have plenty of overpriced junk food. (3) Good fairs must have nauseating rides. (4) Top-drawer fairs must have ridiculous come-ons. (5) Good country fairs must have a "serious" side to them. (6) A four-star carnival must have plenty of "toughs" around. (7) An excellent fair must separate you from your money faster than OPEC and the IRS combined.

(Ronald Wray Boyd, in his review of the Pinellas County Fair for *The St. Petersburg Times,* March 14, 1979. This article also contains Boyd's tips on fair etiquette, offering such timeless bits of advice as, "Don't ask for four cheese dogs, six large Pepsis, three caramel apples and then try to charge it on your Carte Blanche card," and "Don't feel as though you should tip 'The Slime Man.' ")

● **Bradley's Reminder.** Everything comes to him who waits—among other things, death.

(English writer Francis H. Bradley. *ME.*)

● **Brauer's Warning.** He who tries to pick all the flowers is sure to get some poison ivy.

(David F. Brauer, Orlando, Fla.)

● **Brecht's Hierarchy of Needs.** Grub first, then ethics.
(Bertolt Brecht. *RS.*)

● **Brenne's Laws of Life.** (1) You never get it where you want it. (2) If you think it's tough now, just wait.

(From Carol Pike, Mesa, Arizona, who heard them from her father at least once a week during her formative years. She says, "These laws can be applied to anything.")

● **Bressler's Law.** There is no crisis to which academics will not respond with a seminar.

(Professor Marvin Bressler of Princeton University, from Arnold Brown, New York City.)

● **Brewster's Exception.** Every rule has its exceptions except this one: A man must always be present when he is being shaved.

(Eugene V. Brewster, from his 1925 work, *The Wisdom of the Ages.*)

● **Dr. Brochu's Professorial Discourse.** A "full professor" is not an assistant professor, an associate professor, an adjunct professor, or a part-time professor. He has been a professor for a long time, has filled all of his memory circuits with absolutely essential information; he is full of knowledge. *1st Consequence:* He cannot learn anything new without losing some knowledge essential to his position. *2d Consequence:* If he does learn something new, the essential information forgotten as a result of consequence #1 will be requested by the Dean the next time they meet. *3rd Consequence:* If he protects essential knowledge by not learning anything new, a student will ask for the unlearned new knowledge the next day. *4th Consequence:* When the students and administration find out how full he is, he will be promoted to Dean.

(Frank Brochu, M.D., Professor of Surgery, Salem, Va.)

● **Brodie's Law of the Consumption of Canapes.** As many as are served will be eaten . . . if left long enough.

> (Robert N. Brodie, New York City, who points out, "This law applies equally to social and business affairs but operates with special force at new office openings and functions where it is understood that the food costs no individual money.")

● **Brogan's Rules.** (1) When in doubt, blame the schools. (2) Also blame the press.

> (Patrick Brogan, Washington correspondent of *The Times* [London] in a January 14, 1979, article for *The Washington Post.*)

● **Bronx Law of Dominance.** No matter what year it is or how many teams are in the league, the odds are 1:2 that the Yankees will win the pennant. (You could look it up.)

> (Steven D. Mirsky, Ithaca, N.Y.)

● **Brothers's Distinction.** The biggest difference between men and boys is the cost of their toys.

> (Joyce Brothers, quoted in *Bennett Cerf's The Sound of Laughter,* Doubleday, 1970.)

● **Brown's Law of Issues.** Issues are the last refuge of scoundrels.

> (Governor Jerry Brown. *MBC.*)

● **Brozik's Law.** Never ask a question you *really* don't want to know the answer to.

> (Dallas Brozik, Braidwood, Ill.)

● **Bryant's Law.** The toughest stitch on a pair of trousers is that which affixes the price tag.

> (Larry W. Bryant, Arlington, Va.)

BROZIK'S LAW

● **Buchwald's Sans Souci Rules.** (1) Any rumor which survives forty-eight hours is most likely true. (2) When any cabinet officer comes to dine, everyone's lunch is tax deductible.

(Art Buchwald, who formulated them over soft-shell crabs at the Sans Souci Restaurant. They were quoted by Hugh Sidey in his column in *The Washington Star,* February 11, 1979.)

● **Budget Analyst's Rule.** Distribute dissatisfaction uniformly.

(A. A. Lidberg, Tempe, Ariz.)

● **Buechner's Principle.** The simplest explanation is that it doesn't make sense.

(Professor William Buechner, from Richard Stone, Stanford, Cal.)

● **"Bugs" Baer's Perception.** You can always judge a man by what he eats, and therefore a country in which there is no free lunch is no longer a free country.

(Arthur "Bugs" Baer. *ME.*)

● **Bulen's Advice.** Don't put off until tomorrow what you can put off until the day after tomorrow.

(E. H. Bulen, Los Angeles.)

● **Bunuel's Law.** Overdoing things is harmful in all cases, even when it comes to efficiency.

(U/DRW.)

● **Burdg's Philosophy.** It's not the time you put in, but what you put in the time.

(Henry B. Burdg, Auburn, Ala.)

Bureaucratic Survival Kit. Essential Items.

1. Credo of a Bureaucrat.
You start by saying no to requests. Then if you have to go to yes, okay. But if you start with yes, you can't go to no.

(Mildred Perlman revealed this secret when she retired in 1975 as director of classification for New York City's Civil Service Commission.)

2. The Bureaucrat's Ten Commandments.
    I   Don't discuss domestic politics on issues involving war and peace.

ODE TO BUREAUCRATIC IMMORTALITY

II   Say what will convince, not what you believe.
III Support the consensus.
IV   Veto other options.
V   Predict dire consequences.
VI   Argue timing, not substance.
VII Leak what you don't like.
VIII Ignore orders you don't like.
IX   Don't tell likely opponents about a good thing.
X   Don't fight the consensus and don't resign over policy.
(Widely quoted set of instructions by Leslie H. Gelb and Morton M. Halperin.)

3. Ode to Bureaucratic Immortality. When Senator Lawton Chiles of Florida discovered that among the 4,987 forms used by the federal government was one that would be sent to city officials after a nuclear attack asking how many citizens survived, he was moved to comment, "The implication is that even if nothing else survives a nuclear blast, the bureaucracy will rise from the ashes."

4. Useful Motto.
    Do not fix the mistake—fix the *blame.*
        (George Barbarow, Bakersfield, Cal.)

5. Confessions of an IRS Agent (McCoy's Laws).
    (1) If all line sections of government ceased to function, the administrative staff sections would function for three years before they discovered the other sections were gone. (2) Bureaucracy goes beyond the Peter Principle: When someone reaches his highest level of incompetence in a bureaucracy, the only way to get rid of him is to promote him. This continues until he retires or reaches the top of the ladder.
        (Michael P. McCoy, Special Agent, Internal Revenue Service, Criminal Investigation Division, Spring, Tex.)

6. Bureaucrat's Lament.

I had a little document,
   As pure as driven snow,
Yet everywhere that paper went,
   It wandered to and fro.

I thought that people gladly
   And swiftly would concur,
But while I waited sadly,
   They'd cavil and demur.

Some thought the paper much too short;
   Others much too long.
Some thought the language much too weak;
   Others much too strong.

So by the time that document
   Came dawdling back my way
It made no difference where it went—
   The issue was passé!

(U/ Found in a file at the National Aeronautics and Space Administration.)

7. Deliverance.

God told Moses he had good news and bad news.

"The good news first," said Moses.

"I'm planning to part the Red Sea to allow you and your people to walk right through and escape from Egypt," said God, adding, "And when the Egyptian soldiers pursue, I'll send the water back on top of them."

"Wonderful," Moses responded, "but what's the bad news?"

"You write the environmental-impact statement."

    (Oft-told Washington parable, c. 1977.)

8. Brownian Motion Rule of Bureaucracies.

It is impossible to distinguish, from a distance, whether the bureaucrats associated with your project are simply sitting on their hands or frantically trying to cover their asses.

(*U*/ Submitted by Paul Martin to *DRW.*)

● **Burgess's Law of Best Sellers.** A book will sell best if it is very long and very unreadable, since then the buyer feels he is buying a durable commodity. If he races through the book he buys in a single sleepless night, he will feel cheated.

(Anthony Burgess, in *The Washington Post Book World,* April 8, 1979.)

● **Burns's Estimating Formula.** Things cost about a dollar a pound.

(From Martin Berger, Mount Vernon, N.Y., who explains, ''Burns was a college professor from whom I first heard this law. He was also the inventor of the ferrous wheel . . . pictured at right. It has been my observation that this law was surprisingly true over a very long period of time. However, inflation has finally caught up with it; in today's world, two dollars a pound seems closer to the mark.'')

● **Burton's Party Laws.** *I. Children's Birthday Parties.* (1) Any birthday party of more than seven male children under the age of eleven will inevitably end in a fight. (2) Any child's birthday party in which the number of guests exceeds the number of the actual age of the child for whom the party is being given will end in disaster. *II. Adults at Parties.* (1) If a party is scheduled to run from 4 to 7 P.M., then that party will run from 5:30 to 10 P.M.

B

26

(2) If twenty-two people are invited to a party commencing at 9 P.M., one person will invariably turn up at 9 P.M. (3) At any party lasting more than three hours and twenty-two minutes, at least one woman will be crying. (4) At any party catering to more than ten people, at least two glasses will be broken. (5) At any party catering to more than seventeen people, at least four glasses will be broken. (6) At any afternoon party in which the guests stay until after midnight, all glasses will be broken. (7) A wife who has had two drinks on being offered a third will decline it. She will then drink half of her husband's drink. She will then change her mind and say that she would like a third drink. Her husband will drink this drink. (8) Exactly fourteen minutes and seventeen seconds after the host announces that there is nothing more to drink, all guests will leave, no matter what the hour is.

(Pierre Burton, from his book *My War With the 20th Century,* Doubleday, 1965.)

● **Busch's Law of the Forty-Hour Week.** The closer a day is to a weekend, holiday, or vacation, the greater the probability of an employee calling in sick. *Corollary:* No one gets sick on Wednesdays.

(Walter Busch, St. Louis. *EV.*)

Business Maxims. Signs, real and imagined, that belong on the walls of the nation's offices (credits follow the maxims).

* * *

1. Never Try to Teach a Pig to Sing; It Wastes Your Time and It Annoys the Pig.

*   *   *

2.   Sometimes the Crowd Is Right.

*   *   *

3.   Customers Want ¼″ Holes—Not ¼″ Drills.

*   *   *

4.   Dollars Become What You Label Them.

*   *   *

5.   The Real World Is Only a Special Case, Albeit an Important One.

*   *   *

6.   The Easiest Way to Make Money Is to Stop Losing it.

*   *   *

7.   Auditors Are the People Who Go in After the War Is Lost and Bayonet the Wounded.

*   *   *

8.   Criticize Behavior, Not People.

*   *   *

9.   Give More Than They Ask for. More Is Less, but It Looks Like More.

*   *   *

10.   If You Don't Measure It, It Won't Happen.

*   *   *

11.   There Is More Than One Way to Skin a Cat; but Be Sure the Boss Likes Cat.

*   *   *

12. If You Can't Get Your Day's Work Done in Twenty-four Hours—Work Nights.

* * *

13. Whom you Badmouth Today Will Be Your Boss Tomorrow.

* * *

14. Remember, the Key to Success Opens Many Doors.

* * *

15. To Err Is Human—To Forgive Is Not Company Policy.

* * *

16. No Matter How Long the Day May Be, You Cannot Shingle a Roof with Prunes.

* * *

17. Fish Die by Their Mouth.

* * *

18. The Best Way to Get Credit Is to Try to Give It Away.

* * *

19. It Takes Two, but Give Me the Credit.

* * *

20. Even Monkeys Fall from Trees.

* * *

(Many of these maxims were inspired by a collection of business maxims that appeared in *MBA Magazine.* The first four maxims originally appeared in *MBA.* The sources of the other maxims are: number 5, Barry Keating, Assistant Professor of Business Economics, Notre Dame University; 6–8, Paul Rubin, Toledo; 9, Sal Rosa,

New York City; 10, Boake A. Sells, Chagrin Falls, Ohio; 11, B. J. Carroll, Lake Forest, Ill.; 12, Alfred deQuoy, McLean, Va.; 13, S. M. Oddo, San Diego; 14, Seth Frankel, Chicago; 15, E. H. Bulen, Los Angeles; 16, Andrew Weissman, New York City; 17, Ron Wilsie, Solana Beach, Cal.; 18, business leader Charles Hendrickson Brower, quoted in *Reader's Digest,* March 1971; 19, T. Camille Flowers, Cincinnati; 20. Arthur E. Klauser, Washington, D.C.)

● **Butler's Expert Testimony.** The function of the expert is not to be more right than other people, but to be wrong for more sophisticated reasons.
(David Butler, *The Observer,* London.)

● **Butler's Marketing Principle.** Any fool can paint a picture, but it takes a wise man to be able to sell it.
(Samuel Butler.)

● **Buxbaum's Law.** Anytime you back out of your driveway or parking lot, day or night, there will always be a car coming, or a pedestrian walking by.
(*U/JW.*)

● **Byrne's Law of Concreting.** When you pour it rains.
(*U/*Donald Kaul's column in *The Des Moines Register,* December 11, 1978.)

C

● **Caffyn's Law of According To.** The rosier the news the higher ranking the official who announces it.
(H. R. Caffyn, New York City. *AO.*)

● **Callaghan's Answer to the Balance of Payments Problem.** In the 19th century when Britain had defense responsibilities all around the globe, didn't she have balance of payments problems? No, there were no statistics.
(British Prime Minister James Callaghan, in reply to a question at the National Press Club. *TCA.*)

● **Campbell's Constant.** The telephone never rings until you are settled in the bathroom.
(Constance E. Campbell, Keokuk, Iowa.)

● **Campbell's Law.** Nature abhors a vacuous experimenter.
(U/DRW.)

● **Canning's Law.** Nothing is so fallacious as facts, except figures.
(British Prime Minister George Canning, 1770–1827.)

● **Cannon's Razor.** Guys who chew on unlit cigars have a tough time convincing me they're telling the truth.
(Sportswriter Jimmy Cannon.)

● **Capon's Perception.** The world looks as if it has been left in the custody of a pack of trolls.

(Robert Farrar Capon from *The Supper of the Lamb,* Doubleday, 1969. *RS.*)

● **Carlisle's Nursing Keystone.** If you treat a sick child like an adult and a sick adult like a child, everything works out pretty well.

(Ruth Carlisle, quoted in *Reader's Digest,* January 1969.)

● **Carlisle's Rule of Acquisition.** The purchase of any product can be rationalized if the desire to own it is strong enough.

(Carlisle Madson, Hopkins, Minn.)

● **Carlson's Law.** Don't ever try to eat where they don't want to feed you.

(Phil Carlson, long-time Chief of Staff of the Government Operations Committee. It was recited to Jack Sullivan in 1960, when Carlson and Sullivan entered a restaurant in the Canal Zone that refused to serve them. Sullivan suggested they demand to be fed, but Carlson knew better. Sullivan, now a high-ranking State Department official, adds, "I have found many subsequent occasions on which Carlson's Law has seemed quite appropriate.")

● **Carmichael's Law.** For every human reaction there is an over-reaction.

(U/Ra.)

● **Carolyn's Corollary.** A penny saved isn't a hell of a lot.
(David M. Hebertson, Sandy, Utah, who named this for a former girl friend "who did not revel in an 'evening out' at Burger World.")

● **Carroll's Law of Black Box Mechanisms.** If you leave them alone long enough, they will fix themselves. *Corollary 1:*

If they haven't fixed themselves, you haven't left them alone long enough. *Corollary 2:* If you open them up, they will take longer to fix. *Corollary 3:* If you try to fix them, they will be hopelessly beyond repair. *Corollary 4:* If you try to have someone else fix them, it will cost more than a new one.

(B. J. Carroll, Lake Forest, Ill.)

● **Carson's Comedic Laws.** (1) If they buy the premise, they'll buy the bit. (2) Don't do more than three jokes on the same premise.

(Johnny Carson, who has mentioned these laws several times on the *Tonight* show. *MLS.*)

● **Carson's Law of Singularity.** There's only one fruitcake in the whole world.

(Johnny Carson. *MLS.*)

● **Carson's Travel Law.** There is no Gate #1 at any airport.

(Johnny Carson, the *Tonight* show, May 22, 1979.)

● **Carswell's Law of Productivity.** Work smarter, not harder.

(Ron Carswell, Texas State Technical Institute, Waco.)

● **Carter's Rule.** If there is a single puddle in your front yard, the newsboy will hit it, but only on those days when the paper is unwrapped.

(Nelson Carter, Aptos, Cal.)

● **Cason's Laws.** (1) *For Plant Operation:* When in doubt, blame the Maintenance Department. (2) *For Economic Analysis:* The assumption you make without realizing you are making it is the one that will do you in. (3) *For Speed Limitation:* They will remember how poorly the job was done long after they have forgotten how quickly it was done. (4) *For Meetings:* Regardless of the length of the meeting, all important decisions will be made in the last five minutes before lunch or quitting time.

(Roger L. Cason, Wilmington, Del.)

● **Catch-22 Revisited.** A 1969 District of Columbia Court of Appeals decision on Breathalyzer tests rules that for the test to be valid the drunk-driving defendant must be sober enough to give voluntary, informed consent to letting the test be administered.

(Reported in *The Washington Star,* April 16, 1979.)

● **Cavanaugh's Postulate.** All kookies are not in a jar. *(U/DRW.)*

● **Chadwick's Observation on Book Loaning.** The only thing stupider than loaning a book is returning one.

(Clifton Chadwick, Santiago, Chile.)

● **Charlemagne's Rule.** It's smarter to be lucky than it's lucky to be smart.

(Charlemagne, in the musical *Pippin.* Richard Stone, Stanford, Cal.)

● **Cheshire's Law of Social Climbing.** Everything that goes up must come down.

(Maxine Cheshire, *The Washington Post. MLS.*)

● **Chesterton's Discovery.** The only way of catching a train I ever discovered is to miss the train before.

(G. K. Chesterton.)

● **Chesterton's Warning.** Never invoke gods unless you really want them to appear. It annoys them very much.

(G. K. Chesterton, from Sarah Risher, Bethesda, Md.)

● **Chilton's Theological-Clerical Rule.** If you work in a church office you have to keep all your equipment locked up, because nothing is sacred.

(Vee Chilton, Easton, Md.)

● **Christmas Eve, The Primary Myth of.** "So simple that a child can assemble it."

(Side-panel of a toy box that also says, "Some assembly required.")

● **Cicero's Constant.** There is no opinion so absurd but that some philosopher will express it.

(Cicero. *ME.*)

● **Civil Service Maxim. (a.k.a. The Law of the "New Army.")** The pension is mightier than the sword.

(Anonymous. Unsigned note sent to the Murphy Center.)

● **Clark's Law of Leadership.** A leader should not get too far in front of his troops or he will get shot in the ass.

(Senator Joseph S. Clark. *MBC.*)

● **Clarke's Partners Pact Paradox.** You, as one partner, will do 90 percent of the research and 99 percent of the actual term paper. While "he," your partner, will contribute 10 percent of the research and 1 percent of the actual term paper. *Corollary 1:* Of course, the 1 percent of the paper is the title page, and your partner will have spelled your name wrong. *Corollary 2:* In typing the title page your partner will give himself top billing. *Corollary 3:* Your teacher, not knowing of the injustice being done, will give your partner a higher grade than the one he gives you.

(Milo M. Clarke, Cortland, N.Y.)

● **Clay's Conclusion.** Creativity is great, but plagiarism is faster.

(Frederick A. Clay, Anaheim, Cal.)

● **Clayton's Universal Law of Social Evolution.** Bridges prohibit the progress they promote.

> (John S. Clayton, Rockville, Md., who says, "This applies to all churches, school systems, automobiles, television, governments, religions, legal systems, agricultural systems, transportation, modern math, scientific theory, housing development, organizations, social reform, communications systems, political theories, industrial development, labor movements, and the invention of the zipper.")

● **Cliff's Catalog of the Least Credible English Quotations.** (1) The check is in the mail. (2) I'm from the government and I'm here to help you. (3) Of course I'll respect you in the morning.

> *(U/GT.)*

● **Cloninger's Law.** In a country as large as the United States, it is possible to find at least fifty people who will believe/buy/try/or practice anything.

> (Dale O. Cloninger, Associate Professor of Finance and Public Affairs, University of Houston at Clear Lake City.)

● **Close's Clever Cue for Clashing Couples.** If I can prove I'm right, I make things worse.

> (Rev. Henry Close, Fort Lauderdale, Fla., Letters to the Editor, *Time,* March 19, 1979.)

● **Coan's Law.** If it looks complicated, lose interest.
> (Nonnee Coan, Houston.)

● **Coccia's Barbecue Law.** Regardless of where you sit, the wind will always blow the smoke from a barbecue in your face.

> (James R. Coccia, Glens Falls, N.Y., Letters to the Editor, *Time,* March 19, 1979.)

● **Coffin's Revision.** Some folks say the squeaking wheel gets the grease, but others point out that it is the first one to be replaced.

(Harold Coffin, Associated Press.)

● **Cohen's Laws . . .** *Of Candidates:* Many people run for office only because someone they know and don't like is running for the same office. *Of Government Salaries:* Few members of the news media have ever seen a justified pay raise, or even discovered the right time to raise pay or ever learned the right method to raise pay. *Of Political Polling:* Sometimes those who lead in the public opinion polls win the election. *Of Recollections:* Recollections of personal animosities generally last longer than the recollections of the effects of public policies.

(Mark B. Cohen, member, House of Representatives, Commonwealth of Pennsylvania.)

● **Cohodas's Law.** If it looks too good to be true, it is too good to be true.

(Howard L. Cohodas, Marquette, Mich.)

● **Colby's First Rule.** Never burn an uninteresting letter is the first rule of the British aristocracy.

(Frank M. Colby, editor.)

● **Collins's Law of Control.** Businesses exert the tightest controls over the easiest things to control, rather than the most critical.

(Kenneth B. Collins, CBS Publications, New York City.)

● **Collins's Law of Economics.** The cost of living will always rise to exceed income.

(Roger W. Collins, St. Louis. *EV.*)

● **Combs's Laws.** (1) A lot of people who complain about their boss being stupid would be out of a job if he were any smarter. (2) If you think OSHA is a small town in Wisconsin, you're in trouble.

(M. C. "Chuck" Combs, Director, Minnesota Department of Agriculture, Marketing Services. St. Paul, Minn.)

● **Computer Programming Principles.** (1) The computer is never wrong. (2) The programmer is always wrong.

(U/JS.)

● **Congress, Universal Law of.** Neither the House nor the Senate shall pass a law they shall be subject to.

(U/Ra.)

● **Conner's Food Laws.** (1) Whatever the person at the next table orders, it always looks better than yours. (2) All avocados in all stores will always be rock-hard the day you want to make guacamole.

(Caryl Conner, Washington, D.C., Letters to the Editor, *The Washingtonian,* December 1978.)

● **Connor's Restaurant Rule.** The amount of a waiter's or waitress's tip is inversely proportional to the number of people at a table times the amount of time the party occupies the table.

(Kevin Connor, manager, The Man in The Green Hat Restaurant, Washington, D.C. Although Connor admits that this rule is not immutable, he says that it is true enough to prove true at least once or twice on any given day.)

● **Conrad's Rules.** (1) The person who misses the meeting is generally assigned to the work committee. (2) Conscience is that small, inner voice that tells you someone is watching you.

(3) The problem drinker is the one who never buys. (4) One advantage of old age is that there are more younger women all the time.

(Charles Conrad III, Racine, Wisc.)

● **Conservative/Liberal Razor.** A conservative sees a man drowning 50 feet from shore, throws him a 25-foot-long rope, and tells him to swim to it. A liberal throws him a rope 50 feet long, then drops his end and goes off to perform another good deed.

(U/TCA.)

● **Cooch's Law.** (See *Joe Cooch's Law.*)

● **Cook's Theorem.** If you can't solve a problem forward, it can usually be solved by working it backward.

(From Ronald F. Amberger, Staff Chairman, Mechanical Engineering Technology, Rochester Institute of Technology, who says it is named for Professor Cook, his machine-design professor at Rensselaer Polytechnic Institute.)

● **Cooke's Fundamental Theorem of Political Economics.** If you can only cover costs, capitalism is irrelevant.

(Ernest F. Cooke, Chairman, Marketing Department, University of Baltimore.)

● **Cooke's General Business Laws.** (1) Managers with an accounting or legal mentality will take no risk, bend no rules, and the firm will stagnate. (2) The entrepreneur who finds a remarkable new way of financing a company or putting together a conglomerate will be the most surprised when it all falls apart. (3) Just because it works doesn't mean it's right. (4) Just because the industry leader does it that way doesn't mean it's the best way of doing it.

(Ernest F. Cooke again.)

● **Coolidge Collection.** (1) If you don't say anything, you won't be called on to repeat it. (2) Make do, or do without. (3) I've traveled around this country a lot and I'm convinced that there are so many s.o.b.'s in it that they are entitled to some representation in Congress. (In response to an aide's suggestion that Senator so-and-so had gone too far and the president ought to take steps to prevent his renomination.)

(President Calvin Coolidge. *TCA, ME,* Louise Curcio.)

● **Cooper's Law.** All machines are amplifiers.
(U/DRW.)

● **Cooper's Metalaw.** A proliferation of new laws creates a proliferation of new loopholes.
(U/DRW.)

● **Corcoran's Laws.** *Popcorn:* It is impossible to properly salt the lower half of a box of popcorn without oversalting the top half unless you take the saltshaker into the theater with you. *Of Shrinkage:* Everything from your past seems smaller when you see it again except your old flame. *First Law of Sex Laws:* It is more fun trying to think up sex laws than any other laws. *Of Visiting People Who Own a Poodle:* (1) Never visit people who own a poodle. (2) If you do visit people who own a poodle, never throw a ball or small squeak toy to the poodle if you wish to be left alone during the remainder of the visit. *Of Nonsense:* (1) There is no law of nonsense since laws are logical and nonsense is not. Therefore a logical law of nonsense is nonsense and thus not a law. (2) Since the previous law is nonsense, ignore Corcoran's First Law of Nonsense. (3) If you don't like the first two Laws of Nonsense, come up with your own damn Law of Nonsense.

(John H. Corcoran, Jr., Washington, D.C., television personality who also writes good. See also his *Duffer's Laws.*)

● **Corey's Law.** You can get more with a kind word and a gun than you can with a kind word.
(Professor Irwin Corey. *MLS.*)

● **Corporate Survival, First Law of.** Keep your boss's boss off your boss's back.
(U/RA.)

● **Corry's Law.** Paper is always strongest at the perforations.
(U/DRW.)

● **Cossey's Advice.** Instead of starting at the bottom and working up, people should start at the top and work down. Only when one knows the job above can the one below be done correctly.
(Clarence Cossey, Austin, Tex.)

● **Cost Effectiveness, Three Important Points.** (1) The question was raised as to which was the best: (A) a broken watch, or (B) one that ran ten seconds slow per day. A Pentagon cost-effectiveness analysis showed that the broken one was far better. The slow watch will be correct only once every 118 years, whereas the broken one is correct twice per day. (2) The son of a cost-effectiveness specialist bragged to his father that he had saved a quarter by running behind the bus all the way to school. His father complained, "Why didn't you run behind a cab and save $2?" (3) Just before being blasted off into orbit Astronaut Walter Schirra was asked by Dr. E. R. Annis, "What concerns you the most?" Schirra thought and then replied, "Every time I climb up on the couch [in the capsule] I say to myself, 'Just think, Wally, everything that makes this thing go was supplied by the lowest bidder.' "
(FSP.)

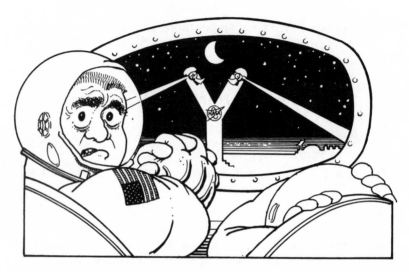

COST EFFECTIVENESS: THIRD IMPORTANT POINT

● **Cotton's Explanation.** One can usually tell from the degree of formality with which one senator refers to another what the nature of their personal relations may be. If the reference is made casually as "Senator Jones," they are probably close friends. If someone refers to a colleague as "the Senator from Michigan," one may infer that they have a cordial relationship. If a senator refers to another as "the distinguished Senator from Indiana," one may assume he does not particularly like him. And if he refers to him as the "very able and distinguished Senator from California," it usually indicates that he hates his guts.

    (Senator Norris Cotton from his book *In The Senate,* Dodd, Mead, 1978.)

● **Court's Laws.** (1) In any country on any given television network or station the quantity and quality of locally produced programs will vary in an inverse proportion to the quantity and quality of old motion pictures transmitted over the same given network or station. (2) If the media are given the opportunity to get the facts wrong, they probably will. (3) When the media make a mistake, the correction will be inversely related to the size and importance of the error.

(Clive Court, Halifax, Nova Scotia.)

● **Craine's Law of Simplicity.** For every simple solution there are a number of complex problems. *Corollary:* For every simple problem there are a number of complex problems.

(Lloyd Craine, Professor and electrical engineer, Pullman, Wash. "This law," he says, "was devised to explain some of the fundamental relationships that escape many laymen and was used during training sessions for persons interested in understanding the energy problem better.")

● **Cramer's Law of the Sea.** You're not really seasick when you are afraid you'll die, but when you're afraid you'll live.

(Les Cramer, Arlington, Va.)

● **Cramer's Law of Teaching.** When you threaten to send the next kid that talks to the office, the next kid that talks will be the best kid in the class.

(Roxanne Cramer, Arlington, Va.)

● **Creamer's Ten Steps to Learning.**
   1. To Learn Is to Hear.
   2. To Hear Is to Listen.
   3. To Listen Is to Speak.
   4. To Speak Is to Think.
   5. To Think Is to Question.
   6. To Question Is to Ponder.
   7. To Ponder Is to Observe.
   8. To Observe Is to See.
   9. To See Is to Be Born.

10. To Be Born Is to Be Screwed.

Moral: Any way you look at it, you've got to get screwed at least once before you learn.

(William P. Creamer, San Ramon, Cal.)

● **Crisp's Creed.** Don't keep up with the Joneses: Drag them down, it's cheaper.

(Quentin Crisp. From Richard Isaac, M.D., Toronto.)

● **Cruickshank's Laws.** *Government:* We have met the enemy: in fact we elected him. *Consumerism:* Never buy a used car from a guy who can talk. Never shop in a place that has "bargain" in its name. *Committees:* If a committee is allowed to discuss a bad idea long enough, it will inevitably vote to implement the idea simply because so much work has already been done on it. *Gambling:* My old Scottish grandfather used to say: "The only game that can't be fixed is peek-a-boo." *Gimme Mine:* No matter how bad the idea, or how poor the results, a program will always be considered a howling success at the local level as long as federal funds continue to pay for it. *Sociology:* Never argue with the bouncer. *Corollary 1:* Never argue with a regular customer—the bouncer always decides in his favor. *Corollary 2:* Stay out of joints that need bouncers unless you plan to be a regular customer.

(Ken Cruickshank, *The Florida Times-Union,* Jacksonville, from his June 25, 1978, column.)

● **Cummings's Rule.** The fish are either shallow, deep, or somewhere in between.

(L. L. Cummings, Professor and Director, Center for the Study of Organizational Performance, University of Wisconsin, Madison.)

● **Cuppy's Evolution of the Species.** All modern men are descended from wormlike creatures, but it shows more on some people.

(Humorist Will Cuppy.)

● **Cureton's Advice.** Avoid jackrabbit starts.
(Stewart Cureton, Jr., Houston.)

● **Custodiet's Complement.** The human hand is made complete by the addition of a baseball.
(U/RA.)

● **Czusack's Law of Design Changes.** Every advantage has a corresponding disadvantage.
(Charlie Czusack, from Ronald F. Amberger, Rochester Institute of Technology.)

D

- **Daniels's Discovery.** The most delightful advantage of being bald—one can *hear* snowflakes.
  (R. G. Daniels, from *Quote . . . Unquote* by Nigel Rees, George Allen and Unwin, 1978.)

- **Darby's Dicta.** (1) If you have to "take it or leave it"—leave it! (2) Every time I finally get an iron in the fire—the fire goes out.
  (*U*/From Mike O'Neill, Citrus Heights, Cal.)

- **Daugherty's Law.** Temporary things tend to become permanent.
  (Richard D. Daugherty, Professor of Anthropology, Washington State University. From Gerald H. Grosso, Port Orchard, Wash.)

- **Daum's Law of Cuckoo Clocks.** At any given party, the cuckoo will always cuckoo at the most embarrassing moment in a conversation.
  (Michael J. Daum, East Chicago, Ind.)

- **Davis's Dictum.** Problems that go away by themselves come back by themselves.
  (Marcy E. Davis, Philadelphia.)

- **Deborkowski's Laundry Law.** If you come out of the Laundromat with an even number of socks, you have somebody else's laundry.
  (*U/Ra.*)

● **DeCicco's Law.** More policemen die in their autos day-dreaming about gunfights than die as a result of gunfights.

    (Alexander DeCicco, Deputy Sheriff, DuPage County, Ill.)

● **Denenberg's Laws.** *Of Rhetorical Effectiveness:* I would measure how effective my speech was by how many hours it took the audience to complain to my employer. *Of Inescapable Elements:* You can't escape death, taxes, or life insurance.

    (Herbert S. Denenberg. *MBC.*)

● **DeQuoy's Catalog of Statements People Will Blindly Accept as Proof of Validity.** (1) It has been computerized. (2) It has been war-gamed.

    (Alfred deQuoy, McLean, Va.)

● **DeRoy's Political Rule.** A politician solves every problem before election but very few after.

    (Richard H. DeRoy, Hilo, Hawaii.)

● **Desk Jockey, Songs of the.** (1) The federal government spends enough in one hour to wire the entire population of North Dakota—and the houses, too. (2) Discriminate as little as you can and still comply with federal regulations. (3) Make the new administrator feel welcome in a Saturday afternoon ceremony. As of Monday morning, he will be behind in his commitments to group X. (4) The principle allegiance of modern man is to his group, which differs from a gang chiefly in that gangs rumble in the streets while groups rumble in the courts and on Capitol Hill. (5) A dresser is a kind of bureau that doesn't tell you how to run your life. (6) The fascination of paper clips grows inversely with the appeal of the work at hand.

    (Ryan Anthony, Tucson.)

● **De Tocqueville's Law.** The lower the calling is and the more removed from learning, the more pompous and erudite is its appellation.

> (Alexis De Tocqueville, *Democracy in America.* From Kevin G. Long, Quebec.)

● **Dial's Discovery.** No matter what you do to instant coffee, it always tastes like instant coffee.

> (Thomas H. Dial, Baltimore.)

● **Dianne's Observation.** If a motel advertises itself as "modern," it isn't.

> (Dianne D. Farrar, Sacramento, Cal.)

● **Dickson's Rules.** *Auto Repair:* If you can see it, it is not serious. If you can hear it, it will set you back some. If you can neither see nor hear it, it will cost you a fortune. *Collecting:* Anything billed as "destined to be a collector's item" (commemorative plates, spoons, Bicentennial kitsch, records sold on late-night TV, etc.) won't be. *Corollary:* Things that aren't, will be. *Telecommunications:* A defective pay phone will find your last dime. *Turnpike Cuisine:* The quality of roadside food decreases in direct proportion to the number of lanes on the road in question. *Insomnia:* (1) Noises, particularly drips and creakings, intensify during the night but abate at dawn. (2) Birds make the most noise at dawn. (3) At the *precise moment* that you *must* get out of bed, there will be absolute quiet. *Transportation:* The bigger the terminal, the worse the public address system. *American Studies:* There is no phenomenon so small that some professor, writer, or politician will not latch on to it and declare that it signifies a turning point in American history. *Defense Language:* The more innocuous the name of a weapon, the more hideous its impact. (Some of the most horrific weapons of the Vietnam era were named BAMBI, INFANT, Daisycutter, Grasshopper, and Agent Orange. Nor is the trend new: From the past we have Mustard Gas, Angel Chasers (two cannonballs linked with a chain

DICKSON'S RULE OF COLLECTING

for added destruction), and the Peacemaker, to name a few.) *Roadside Economics:* Places with the suffix "-tronics" or the word "systems" in their name will charge more for the same goods or service than places with "Mr." or "City" in their name (as in Mr. Carwash or Clean City.) But forced K's (as in Kwick and Klean) aren't as cheap as they look. If you really want to overpay for something, try an antique shop with a crude, hand-lettered sign with the "n" written backward. Stores with first names (John's, Fred's, Maxine's) are generally cheaper than those with last names (Bloomingdale's, Tiffany's, Brooks Brothers, etc.). *Suburban Development:* The more trees a developer cuts down, the woodsier the name of the resulting housing development.

(Paul Dickson, Director, The Murphy Center.)

● **Disney World Rule.** Children under twelve must be accompanied by money.

(James Dent, Charleston [W. Va.] *Gazette.*)

● **Disraeli's Maxims.** (1) A precedent embalms a principle. (2) In politics, nothing is contemptible.

(Benjamin Disraeli.)

● **Dmitri's Epigrams.** (1) Nobody can ever get too much approval. (2) No matter how much you want or need, *they,* whoever *they* are, don't want to let you get away with it, whatever *it* is. (3) Sometimes you get away with it.

(John Leonard, who sometimes calls himself Dmitri in his *New York Times* columns. From his column.)

● **Dochter's Dictum.** Somewhere, right now, there's a committee deciding your future; only you weren't invited.

(U/NDB.)

● **Don Marquis's Advice to Writers.** If you want to get

rich from writing, write the sort of thing that is read by persons who move their lips when they are reading to themselves.

(Don Marquis, quoted by Franklin P. Adams in his book *Overset,* Doubleday, 1922.)

● **Donna's Law of Purchase.** If you want it, and can afford it, buy it—it won't be there when you go back.

(Donna P. H. Day, Rock Hill, Mo.)

● **Dowd's Bath Principle.** It takes more hot water to make cold water hot than it takes cold water to make hot water cold.

(Larry G. Dowd, Columbia, Mo.)

● **Dowling's First Law of Hollywood Moviemaking.** No truly bad movie gets that way without consciously attempting to join (or initiate) a trend.

(Tom Dowling, *The Washington Star,* July 30, 1978.)

● **Drogin's Mealtime Maxim.** A balanced meal is whatever gets hot all at the same time. A snack is what doesn't.

(Marc Drogin, Roanoke [Va.] *World-News,* March 23, 1965.)

● **Drunk, Rules for Getting.** (1) Not too often. (2) In good company. (3) With good wine.

(From *In Praise of Drunkenness* by Boniface Oinophilus, published in London in 1812. The author marshals strong proof for each of his rules. For instance, in support of the second rule, he says, "A man in former times would have done very ill to get drunk with Heliogabalus, whose historian reports that, after having made his friends drunk, he used to shut them up in an apartment, and at night let loose upon them lions, leopards, and tigers, which always tore to pieces some of them.")

● **Duffer's Laws.** (1) No matter how bad a round of golf you play, there will always be at least one stroke so perfect, so on target, and so gratifying that you will come back to play again. (2) The best way for a Duffer to go around a tree standing directly in his line is to aim directly at the tree, since you never hit where you're aiming anyway. (3) The only time you'll hit the ball straight is when you're applying Duffer's law #2. (4) Never carry more clubs than you can afford to break. (5) It is a myth that playing an old ball guarantees you will carry the lake. (6) Nobody cares what you shot today, except you.

(John H. Corcoran, Jr., Chevy Chase, Md.)

● **Dukes's Law.** The most powerful words in marketing are "Watch this!"

(From James A. Robertson, El Paso, who learned it from Carlton Dukes, Dallas.)

● **Dumas's Law.** Most general statements are false, including this one.

(Alexander Dumas. From John C. Armor, Baltimore.)

● **Dyer's Observation.** It all boils down to two words: "Send money," or "Raise dues," or "Increase taxes."

(Professor John M. Dyer, director, International Finance and Marketing Program, University of Miami, Coral Gables.)

E

● **Earle's Law of Relativity.** The shortest period of time is that between when the light turns green and when the guy behind you blows his horn.

(M. Mack Earle, Baltimore.)

● **Edison's Axiom.** We don't know one-millionth of one percent about anything.

(Thomas Alva Edison. *GT.*)

● **Editorial Laws.** (1) When you proudly publish a . . . significant article and expect a large reader response, you'll get one letter telling you about a typo in the third paragraph. (2) A dangling participle deserves dangling. (3) The poorer the writer the greater his resistance to editorial changes. (4) The author best qualified to write a special article on a hot topic is always away on a three-month overseas assignment. (5) During an interview with an important . . . official, the point of your pencil will break off at the most quotable quote. (6) If you create a magazine that is so good that subscribers refuse to part with it—that's bad. If, however, you put out a magazine that means so little to each individual that it gets passed from hand to hand, that's good. For advertisers, that is. (7) Never expect a good writer to be a good editor; never expect a former English teacher to be a good writer; or a former typing teacher to be a good manuscript typist. (8) When an article reference and page number are given on your magazine cover, the page number will change before the magazine goes to press.

(Selected from *Edpress News,* published by the Educational Press Association of America. Laws 1–6 are by the

Edpress editor Ben Brodinsky, the next is by "Editorial Experts," Washington, D.C., and the final law is by Walter Graves, *Today's Education.*)

● **Edwards's Laws.** (1) A telephone number is not recorded on the message unless you already know it. (2) Always carry a pen. (3) . . . .

> Go Ivy League?
> I sure won't
> My shirts taper
> But I don't.

(Robert V. Edwards, Washington, D.C.)

● **Edwards's Tautology.** Fat men are good-natured because good-natured men are usually fat.
(Canadian editor/humorist Bob Edwards.)

Special Section 3

On Efficiency.

An Efficiency Expert Reports on Hearing a Symphony at the Royal Festival Hall in London.

For considerable periods, the four oboe players had nothing to do. The number should be reduced and the work spread more evenly over the whole of the concert, thus eliminating peaks of activity.

All the twelve violins were playing identical notes; this seems unnecessary duplication. The staff of this section should be drastically cut. If a larger volume of sound is required, it could be obtained by electronic apparatus.

Much effort was absorbed in the playing of demi-semi-quavers; this seems to be an unnecessary refinement. It is recommended that all notes should be rounded up to the nearest semiquaver. If this was done it would be possible to use trainees and lower-grade operatives more extensively.

There seems to be too much repetition of some musical passages. Scores should be drastically pruned. No useful purpose is served by repeating on the horns a passage that has already been handled by the strings. It is estimated that if all redundant passages were eliminated, the whole concert time of two hours could be reduced to twenty minutes and there would be no need for an intermission.

The conductor agrees generally with these recommendations, but expressed the opinion that there might be some falling off in box-office receipts. In that unlikely event it should be possible to close sections of the auditorium entirely, with a consequential saving of overhead expenses, lighting, attendance, etc. If the worst came to the worst, the whole thing could be abandoned and the public could go to the Albert Hall instead.

(The Murphy Center has received a number of versions of this report, which was obviously created in England. One Fellow says he first saw a copy in London in 1955.)

● **Einstein's Explanation of Relativity.** Sit with a pretty girl for an hour, and it seems like a minute; sit on a hot stove for a minute, and it seems like an hour—that's relativity.
(Albert Einstein. *ME.*)

● **Einstein's Three Rules of Work.** (1) Out of clutter find simplicity. (2) From discord make harmony. (3) In the middle of difficulty lies opportunity.

(Albert Einstein, quoted in *Newsweek,* March 12, 1979.)

● **Eisenstein's Laws of Tourism.** (1) If you go during the season with the best weather, it will be the worst weather in forty-nine years. (2) No matter where you sit, the view out the other side will be better. (3) If you move from a room into another one because something is wrong, something will be worse in the new room. (4) The best trips are the unplanned ones; this way, you won't worry about fouling up your timetable. Conversely, the tighter the timetable, the more you'll worry and the later you'll be.

(Edward L. Eisenstein, University City, Mo.)

● **Eldridge's Explanation of War.** Man is always ready to die for an idea, provided that idea is not quite clear to him.

(Paul Eldridge, quoted in *Reader's Digest,* February 1963.)

● **Emergency Rule.** IN CASE OF ATOMIC ATTACK, THE FEDERAL RULING CONCERNING PRAYER IN THIS BUILDING WILL BE TEMPORARILY SUSPENDED.

(Sign [handwritten] found posted in a federal office building, Washington, D.C.)

● **Emery's Law.** Regulation is the substitution of error for chance.

(Fred J. Emery, Director, *The Federal Register,* Washington, D.C.)

Special Section 4

Energy Matters.

1. How You Can Save with a Wood Stove.

Stove, pipe, installation, etc.	$458.00
Chain saw	149.95
Care and maintenance for chain saw	44.60
4-wheel-drive pickup, stripped	8,379.04
4-wheel-drive pickup maintenance	438.00
Replace rear window of pickup (twice)	310.00
Fine for cutting unmarked tree in state forest	500.00
Fourteen cases Michelob	126.00
Littering fine	50.00
Towing charge—truck from creek	50.00
Doctor's fee for removing splinter from eye	45.00
Safety glasses	29.50
Emergency-room treatment (broken toes— dropped logs)	125.00
Safety shoes	49.95
New living room carpet	800.00
Paint living room walls and ceiling	110.00
Log splitter	150.00
Fifteen-acre woodlot	9,000.00
Taxes on woodlot	310.00
Replace coffee table (chopped up and burned while drunk)	75.00
Divorce settlement	33,678.22
Total first year's cost	54,878.26
Savings in conventional fuel first year	(72.33)
Net cost of first year's woodburning	$54,805.93

(From ME.)

2. Best One-Liner on the Energy Crisis.
If God had meant for us to have enough oil he never would
have given us the Department of Energy.
(Robert Orben.)

● **Epperson's Law.** When a man says it's a silly, childish
game, it's probably something his wife can beat him at.
(Don Epperson, quoted in Bill Gold's District Line column
in *The Washington Post,* September 11, 1978.)

● **Epstean's Laws.** (1) Man always tends to satisfy his needs
and desires with the least possible exertion. (2) If self-preserva-
tion is the first law of human conduct, exploitation is the second.
(Edward Epstean, from Albert Jay Nock's *Memoirs of a
Superfluous Man,* Regnery, 1964. *JMcC.*)

● **The ERDA Law of Materials Procurement.** Never use
lead when gold will do.
(U/GT.)

● **Erickson's Law of the Sea.**
When in doubt, go fast;
When in danger, go faster.
(L. Bruce Erickson. *MLS.*)

● **Ertz's Observation on Immortality.** Millions long for
immortality who do not know what to do with themselves on a
rainy Sunday afternoon.
(Author Susan Ertz.)

Special Section 5

Explanations. A small catalog of previously eluded truths.

1. Why America's Bicentennial was not more spectacular.
Because the late Wernher von Braun's suggestion to the Senate Space Committee was not adopted. In September 1969 he proposed putting the President of the United States in orbit to celebrate the two-hundredth anniversary of the Republic.

2. Why one should not be too afraid of the Internal Revenue Service.
Recently the IRS demanded that Elizabeth R. Tunnel of Norfolk, Va., pay tax on the many automobiles that the government had determined were in her possession. Ms. Tunnel is the Elizabeth River Tunnel that runs beneath the Elizabeth River. The cars are not hers.

3. Why metric conversion is going to take a lot longer than previously anticipated.
As one radio preacher is reported to have stated, "If God had meant for us to go metric, why did he give Jesus twelve disciples?"

4. Why the United States uses humans in space.
"Man," says a 1965 NASA report on manned space, "is the lowest-cost, 150-pound, nonlinear, all-purpose computer system which can be mass-produced by unskilled labor."

5. Why television is not living up to its promise as an educational medium.

The following was actually edited out of the Nixon-Frost TV interviews:

RN: . . . We were sitting in the bow of the yacht. I'm an old Navy man. The bow is the rear-end, isn't it?

DF: . . . I, ah, . . . probably.

RN: That's right. No. The stern. We were sitting in the stern.

DF: Let's say end.

RN: All right. We were sitting down at the end of the yacht.

6. *Why the government has such a hard time getting out of things it has gotten into.*

Here is how the term "exit" has been defined by government experts:

An exit is a means of egress and has three component parts.

First, an exit access: Exit access is that portion of a means of egress which leads to an entrance to an exit.

Second, the exit itself: Exit is that portion of a means of egress which is separated from all other spaces of the building or structure by construction or equipment as required in this subpart to provide a protected way of travel to the exit discharge.

Third, the exit discharge: That portion of a means of egress between the termination of an exit and a public way.

- **Fadiman's Law of Optimum Improvement.** In the realm of objects, as well as in the realm of ethics, there can be an excess of refinement as well as a defect of crudity. It is my further conviction that a proper technological society is not the one capable of endlessly improving its artifacts, but the one able to see at what point it is best, from the point of view of the whole human being (and indeed of the whole human race), to stop the improvement.

(Clifton Fadiman, from *This Is My Funniest,* edited by Whit Burnett, Perma Books, 1957. In his essay of the same title as the law, Fadiman gives many examples of "excessive refinement," but one that serves as well as any is book wrapping. He notes that books used to come wrapped in a piece of paper tied with a piece of cord. "In no time you could be reading the book." Now he points out, they come in "cardboard iron maidens, suitable to the transportation of safes or pianos" or in "thick bags" that are almost impossible to open without ripping. When ripped, "Out flies a bushel of ancient furry shredded gray paper, the perfect stand-in for mouse dirt.")

- **Family Law.**
  Where there's a sibling
  There's quibbling.
  (Selma Raskin. It originally appeared in *The Wall Street Journal* and is quoted in Charles Preston's *The Light Touch.*)

- **Fannie's Ganif Theory.** (1) Most politicians are thieves. (2) Most politicians are slow learners. (3) Therefore, never vote for an incumbent. While the challenger's natural inclinations are equally bad, it will take him time to learn how to achieve his goals.

(From Carl T. Bogus, Philadelphia, who attributes it to his Aunt Fannie, Mrs. Fagel Kanev.)

● **Faraday's Lecture Rule.** One hour is long enough for anyone.

(Scientist Michael Faraday.)

● **FCC "Policy."** Any sufficiently promising technology must be regulated or it will succeed.

(R. W. Johnson, from his *Ham Radio Humor,* 1977.)

● **Feather's Discovery.** Loneliness is something you can't walk away from.

(William Feather. *RS.*)

● **Feazel's Rules:** *Travel.* Don't Go Back! It isn't there anymore. Exception: Switzerland. *Family Life:* Once you have trained your children to be an efficient team, they go away. (Examples: haying, sailing, fence building, automotive maintenance, cooking, bridge, firewood procurement.) *Experience:* You never learn anything useful from your mistakes because you never get a chance to make the same one twice. *Jogging:* All hilly courses are uphill both ways.

(Betty Feazel, Pagosa Springs, Colo.)

● **Feline Frustration, Rule of.** When your cat has fallen asleep on your lap and looks utterly content and adorable, you will suddenly have to go to the bathroom.

(U/DRW.)

● **Field's Advertising Observation.** People who think that newspaper advertisements are not read should watch a man sitting in a streetcar where women are standing.

(Chester Field, Jr., from his *Cynic's Rules of Conduct* [1905].)

● **Fields's Panaceas.** (1) If at first you don't succeed try, try again. Then quit. There's no use making a fool of yourself. (2) The best cure for insomnia is to get a lot of sleep.

(W. C. Fields.)

● **Fields's Revelation.** If you see a man holding a clipboard and looking official, the chances are good that he is supposed to be doing something menial.

(Wayne C. Fields, Jr., Newcastle, Cal.)

● **Figley's Law.** The price of a hamburger is in inverse proportion to its state of assembly.

(Preston Figley, Rudder & Finn, Texas. *AO.*)

● **The First Time—Each Time Is Like—Law.** No matter how many times you have felt miserable because you stayed up too late, drank too much, ate too much, etc., the next time you have the opportunity to stay up late, drink too much, etc., you will be unable to recall and anticipate, as anything more than an abstraction, how miserable you felt/will feel when you did/if you do. Exception: anything that resulted in carsickness.

(Hilde Weisert, Teaneck, N.J.)

● **Fitzmaurice's Law.** When you come to a stop sign and can't decide whether to turn right or left, any decision will be wrong.

(Richard Fitzmaurice, KCBS, San Francisco.)

● **Flak Diversion Theorem.** A published remark by any congressman that irritates a lobbying association or the White

House is automatically labeled by his office as "taken out of context."

(*The Washington Star* editorial, February 18, 1979.)

● **Florio's Travel Suggestion.** If you will be a traveler, have always the eyes of a falcon, the ears of an ass, the face of an ape, the mouth of a hog, the shoulders of a camel, the legs of a stag, and see that you keep two bags very full, one of patience and another of money.

(A man named John Florio, who wrote the above in 1591. Quoted in the Summer 1978 issue of *J. D. Journal.*)

● **Followers' Creed.** The lemmings know something we don't.

(Alvin W. Quinn, Arlington Heights, Ill.)

● **Fonda's Cinematic Distinction.** If a man and a woman go into the woods with a picnic basket and a blanket and have a picnic, that's a G. If they go into the woods with a picnic basket and crawl under the blanket, that's a PG. And if they go into the woods without a basket or a blanket and have a picnic anyway, that's an R.

(Jane Fonda, 1978 Academy Awards ceremony.)

● **Forbes's Rule of Parenting.** Let your children go if you want to keep them.

(Malcolm Forbes, *The Sayings of Chairman Malcolm,* Harper & Row, 1978.)

● **Fortune-Seeker's Law.** Cast your bread on the water and you get soggy bread.

(U/Ra.)

● **Fowler's Note.** The only imperfect thing in nature is the human race.

(U/DRW.)

● **The Fox Epiphenomenon.** If you do nothing, nothing will happen. If you do something, something will happen—but not what you intended.

(James F. Fox, New York City.)

● **France's Law of Law.** The law, in its majestic equality, forbids the rich as well as the poor to sleep under bridges, to beg in the streets, and to steal bread.

(Anatole France.)

● **Frankel's Principle.** Always think of something new; this helps you forget your last rotten idea.

(Seth Frankel, Hillsdale, N.J.)

● **Franklin's Infallible Remedy for Toothache.** Wash the root of the aching tooth in vinegar, and let it dry half an hour in the sun.

(Benjamin Franklin.)

● **Fresco's Discovery.** If you knew what you were doing, you'd probably be bored.

(Catherine B. Fresco, Winston-Salem, N.C.)

● **Fri's Laws of Regulatory Agencies.** (1) If any agency can regulate, it will. (2) Regulation drives out broad-gauged, long-term thinking.

(Robert Fri, former Environmental Protection Administrator. *AO.*)

● **Fried's Third Law of Public Administration.** If it's logical, rational, reasonable, and makes good common sense, it's not done. *Corollary:* If it's logical, rational, reasonable, and makes good common sense, don't you do it!

(Steve Fried, Ohio Department of Economic and Community Development, Columbus.)

● **Friedman's Law of Elevators.** The amount of time an elevator takes in arriving is directly proportional to the lateness of the person waiting for it, and inversely proportional to the amount of weight in that person's arms. *Corollary:* In a crowded elevator, the person getting off first is at the back of the elevator.

(Robert J. Friedman, Lansdale, Pa.)

● **Frost's Working Rule.** By working faithfully eight hours a day, you may eventually get to be a boss and work twelve hours a day.

(Robert Frost.)

● **Fuchs's Warning.** If you actually look like your passport photo, you aren't well enough to travel.

(Sir Vivian Fuchs. *MLS.*)

● **Fuller's Historical Explanation.** In some cases, people were as much a part of the problem as anybody else.

(A professor of the same name who uttered this and other statements of this type, thereby causing Steve Cohen, Ithaca, N.Y., to drop the class.)

● **Fullner's Rules:** *Consumerism:* Regardless of who or what is responsible for inflationary increases in the cost of goods and services, the consumer pays. *Social Investment:* A male altering his personal behavior, mannerisms, grooming, etc., to accommodate a female of his attention will, subsequent to the termination of the relationship or acquaintance, meet another receptive female whose preferences concur with his characteristics prior to transformation. *Weekends:* Whenever the only time available to complete a task is on weekends, all suppliers of necessary parts, material, and equipment will be open for business Monday through Friday.

(Randall Fullner, San Jose, Cal.)

G

● **Galbraith's Law of Human Nature.** Faced with the choice between changing one's mind and proving that there is no need to do so, almost everybody gets busy on the proof.

> (John Kenneth Galbraith, quoted in Andrea Williams's *Economics, Peace and Laughter,* Houghton Mifflin.)

● **Ganci's Advice.** You can tell a person they're ugly. You can tell a person their feet smell. You can even insult their mother, but never, never, never tell them they're stupid.

> (Jerome G. Ganci, Brooklyn, N.Y.)

● **Gandhi's Observation.** There is more to life than increasing its speed.

> (Mahatma Gandhi.)

● **Garland's Law.** One man's tax break is another man's tax increase.

> (Virginia legislator Ray Garland, quoted in *The Washington Post,* February 12, 1979.)

● **Generalization.** Generally speaking, it is dangerous to generalize.

> (Michael J. Wagner, St. Albert, Alberta, who says, "I have been told that this truth originated in one of the general organizations, i.e., General Motors, General Electric, General Tire . . .")

● **Gerrold's Law of Book Publishing.** You always find teh one typo in print that you missed in galleys.

(David Gerrold, Hollywood, Cal. See also *Short's Quotations.*)

● **Getty's Lament.** In some ways a millionaire just can't win. If he spends too freely, he is criticized for being extravagant and ostentatious. If, on the other hand, he lives quietly and thriftily, the same people who would have criticized him for being profligate will call him a miser.
(J. Paul Getty, quoted in *Forbes,* November 13, 1978.)

● **Getty's Second Law.** If you know how much you are worth, you are not worth much.
(J. Paul Getty, from Clifton Chadwick, Santiago, Chile.)

● **Giamatti's Rule of Choice.** It is my experience, in planning a course of study or anything else, that the person soonest sad, and who laments the longest, is the person who has only the courage of other people's convictions.
(Angelo Bartlett Giamatti, President, Yale University, quoted in *The Boston Globe,* November 12, 1978.)

● **Gillette's Principle.** If you want to make people angry, lie. If you want to make them absolutely livid with rage, tell the truth.
(Robert D. Gillette, M.D., Director, Riverside Family Practice Center, Toledo.)

● **Gingras's Distinction.** There is a difference between bending over backward and bending over forward.
(Armando R. Gingras, Boulder, Colorado.)

● **Ginsburg's Law.** The team you root for will always have a better season the year after you stop rooting for it.
(Phil Ginsburg, Concord, N.H.)

● **Glass's Law.** Enough money is always $5,000 more than I make.

(U/Ra.)

● **Gleason's Advice to Public Administrators.** When leaving office, give your successor three sealed envelopes and instructions to open them in order as crises occur in the new administration. The message in the first should read "blame it on your predecessor," the second should read "announce a major reorganization," and the third should say, "write out three envelopes for your successor."

(James Gleason, on leaving the post of County Executive, Montgomery County, Md. Quoted in *The Montgomery Journal*, November 24, 1978.)

● **Gloom of Night Law.** Checks are always delayed in the mail; bills arrive on time or sooner.

(U/Donald Kaul's column in *The Des Moines Register*, December 11, 1978.)

Special Section 6

Glossary of Important Business Terms. *(For anyone who works in an office.)*

● *Activate.* To make carbons and add more names to the memo.
● *Advanced Design.* Beyond the comprehension of the ad agency's copywriters.
● *All New.* Parts not interchangeable with existing models.
● *Approved, Subject to Comment.* Redraw the damned thing.

FORWARDED FOR YOUR CONSIDERATION

● *Automatic.* That which you can't repair yourself.

● *Channels.* The trail left by interoffice memos.

● *Clarify, To.* To fill in the background with so many details that the foreground goes underground.

● *Conference, A.* A place where conversation is substituted for the dreariness of labor and the loneliness of thought.

● *Confidential Memorandum.* No time to mimeograph/photocopy for the whole office.

● *Consultant.* Someone who borrows your watch to tell you what time it is—then walks away with the watch.

● *Coordinator.* The person who has a desk between two expediters (see *Expedite*).

● *Developed After Years of Intensive Research.* Discovered by accident.

● *Expedite.* To confound confusion with commotion.

● *Forwarded for your Consideration.* You hold the bag for a while.

- *FYI.* Found Yesterday, Interested?
- *Give Someone the Picture, To.* To make a long, confused and inaccurate statement to a newcomer.
- *Give Us the Benefit of Your Present Thinking.* We'll listen to what you have to say as long as it doesn't interfere with what we've already decided to do.
- *In Conference.* Nobody can find him/her.
- *In Due Course.* Never.
- *Infrastructure.* (1) The structure within an infra. (2) The structure outside the infra. (3) A building with built-in infras.
- *It Is in Process.* So wrapped up in red tape that the situation is almost hopeless.
- *Let's Get Together on This.* I'm assuming you're as confused as I am.
- *Note and Initial.* Let's spread the responsibility for this.
- *Policy.* We can hide behind this.
- *Program, A.* Any assignment that cannot be completed by one telephone call.
- *See me.* Come down to my office, I'm lonely.
- *Sources.*
    - ■*Reliable Source*—The person you just met.
    - ■*Informed Source*—The person who told the person you just met.
    - ■*Unimpeachable Source*—The person who started the rumor originally.
- *Top Priority.* It may be idiotic, but the boss wants it.
- *Under Active Consideration.* We're looking in the files for it.
- *Under Consideration.* Never heard of it.
- *We Are Making a Survey.* We need more time to think of an answer.
- *We Will Look into It.* By the time the wheel makes a full turn, we assume you will have forgotten about it too.
- *Will Advise in Due Course.* If we figure it out, we'll let you know.

(Compiled from several sets of "Office Definitions" re-
trieved from real offices.)

● **Godin's Law of the Sexual Revolution.** Sex is here to
stay but it will never be the same.
>(Guy Godin, Université Laval, Quebec. From his unpub-
>lished paper, "The Five or Six Ages of Sex.")

● **Goldberg's Law.** If anything can be misconstrued about
the Jews, it will be . . . and has been.
>(M. Hirsh Goldberg, author of *Just Because They're Jew-
>ish,* Stein & Day, 1978. Quoted in an interview in the
>*Baltimore News American,* January 31, 1979. *ME.*)

● **Golden Rule Revised I.** Do unto others . . . then split.
>*(U/Ra.)*

● **Golden Rule Revised II.** Whatsoever you would laugh
at in others, laugh at in yourself.
>(Harry Emerson Fosdick, from his book *On Being a Real
>Person,* Harper, 1943.)

● **Goldwynism, Tenets of.** (1) Every director bites the
hand that lays the golden egg. (2) If you can't give me your word
of honor, will you give me your promise? (3) Why only *twelve*
disciples? Go out and get thousands! (4) Who wants to go out and
see a bad movie when they can stay at home and see a bad one
free on TV?
>(Attributed to Samuel Goldwyn, various sources.)

● **Golfing: Observations, Theories, and Additional
Rules.** (1) Rail-splitting produced an immortal president in
Abraham Lincoln; but golf, with 29,000 courses, hasn't produced

even a good A-Number-1 congressman. (2) Man blames fate for other accidents but feels personally responsible for a hole in one. (3) Golf is a form of work made expensive enough for rich men to enjoy. It is physical and mental exertion made attractive by the fact that you have to dress for it in a $200,000 clubhouse. Golf is what letter-carrying, ditch-digging, and carpet-beating would be if those tasks could be performed on the same hot afternoon in short pants and colored socks by gouty looking gentlemen who required a different implement for each mood. (4) In arriving at a judgment on whether or not ground is under repair for purpose of lifting a ball unpleasantly situated without penalty, the player shall toss a coin. If it falls, the ground may be deemed under repair. (5) A ball striking a tree while in flight shall be deemed not to have struck a tree unless the player making the stroke declares that he was deliberately aiming for it. In this case, play shall cease momentarily while his partners congratulate him on his marksmanship. But if the player attests in good faith that it was in no sense his intention to strike the tree, then it is obviously a piece of bad luck that has no place in a scientific game. No penalty shall accrue to the player, who is thereupon permitted to estimate the distance his ball would have traveled, but no more than half the distance to the goal line, or two bases.

(Various sources: [1] Will Rogers. [2] *Horizons* magazine. [3] *Essex Golf and Country Club News.* [4 and 5] Mimeographed unattributed "Rules of Golf" from *ME.*)

● **Gomez's Law.** If you don't throw it, they can't hit it. ("Lefty" Gomez.)

● **Gonzalez's Laws.** (1) The easiest way to change a typewriter ribbon is to go out and buy a new typewriter. (2) If you call and they say "the check is in the mail," be prepared to call them a week later and the week after that. (3) Your enemies always photograph better than you.

(Gloria Gonzalez, West New York, N.J.)

● **Goodman's Resolution.** To keep a little more "less" in this new year.

> (Ellen Goodman, from her nationally syndicated column of September 12, 1978.)

● **Gooen's Laws of Lost Energy.** (1) If it takes one person one hour to do a specific job, it will take two hours for two people to do the same job. (2) If it takes one person an hour to hike 2 miles on a trail, it will take two people an hour and a half to cover that same distance.

> (Irwin Gooen, Oneonta, N.Y.)

● **Gordon's Law.** If you think you have the solution, the question was poorly phrased.

> (Robert Gordon, East Granby, Conn.)

● **Gotwald's Law of Behavior Modification.** When a kick in the ass doesn't work, create envy.

> (Rev. Frederick G. Gotwald, Syracuse, N.Y.)

● **Gould's Two-Shirt Theory of Arctic Exploration.** Wear the first shirt until it becomes unbearable; then switch to the second shirt. Wear the second shirt until *it* becomes unbearable (by which time the first shirt will look pretty good again). This process may be repeated indefinitely.

> *(U/GT.)*

● **Governor's Rule.** Everyone at the executive end of Pennsylvania considers everyone at the congressional end an s.o.b. and vice versa. The governors consider anyone from Washington an s.o.b. no matter which end of the avenue he comes from.

> (Discovered by *TCA* when representing the Executive Branch at the Governors' Conference in Colorado Springs, 1949.)

● **Gracy's Axiom.** Don't pay duty. It is such a waste; the government has got more money than is good for it already and would only spend it.

(A lady in P. G. Wodehouse's novel *The Luck of the Bodkins* [London, 1935], explaining why she wants an expensive necklace smuggled through customs. Used by columnist George Will to explain the passage of Proposition 13 in California.)

● **Grammatical Exclusion Principle.** If it can be said clearly, plainly, and in English it has just as logical and valid a claim for being examined as any other similarly constructed statement.

(From an unsigned article of the same name in the July 1963 issue of *Air Force/Space Digest.* The gist of the article is that the author came up with this conclusion after making a tongue-in-cheek but well-worded proposal regarding an Air Force satellite. Later he found the Air Force had adopted his idea—in fact, it had become central to their planning.)

● **Grant's Musical Distinction.** I know two tunes: one of them is "Yankee Doodle," and the other isn't.
(Ulysses S. Grant.)

● **Grants Chant.**

> Pull up your socks!
> Hitch up your pants!
> Get in there and fight for
> Your Federal grants!

(Senator Harry F. Byrd, Jr., recited this on the floor of the U.S. Senate on October 3, 1974. He was protesting the hundreds of thousands of dollars in research money going to Harvard and Yale and suggested that this be used as a cheer at the Harvard-Yale football game.)

● **Gray's Theorems:** *Of N+2.* The number of referred papers required to obtain tenure in an American university is N +2, independent of the number N that have already been published. *Of the Sacrificial Victim.* Nothing gets done in America until somebody dies.

(Paul Gray, Professor, School of Business Administration, University of Southern California. He explains, "The first is based on watching tenure review committees for a number of years. The second has some classic examples: drug safety legislation was required by the Thalidomide disaster; exact fare was put in on buses after several drivers were killed; the FAA's R&D budget goes up after each major crash and then declines; pollution became a seriously recognized problem after Donora.")

● **Great, Rule of the.** When someone you greatly admire and respect appears to be thinking deep thoughts, they are probably thinking about lunch.
(U/DRW.)

● **Great American Axiom.** Some is good, more is better. Too much is just right.
(U/Ra.)

● **Greenfield's Rule of Practical Politics.** Everybody is for democracy—in principle. It's only in practice that the thing gives rise to stiff objections.
(Meg Greenfield, *The Washington Post,* in an article entitled "The People's Revenge," June 14, 1978.)

● **Greenhaus's Summation.** I'd give my right arm to be ambidextrous.
(U/DRW.)

● **Greenyea's Advice.** Learn to clip your fingernails with your left hand because you might not always have your right.
    (Writer John Greenyea, Kensington, Md., who learned this from his late father.)

● **Griffith's Maxim.** If it makes you nervous, don't watch. (Jean Sharon Griffith, Vice President of Student Services, Richland College, Dallas.)

● **Grizzly Pete's Philosophy.** (1) Don't do nothin' too much. (2) When a man gives you his reason for an act, just remember the chances are, nine out of ten, the reason is a trail blinder. (3) The most successful liar is the one who lies the least. (4) If there is anything in the theory of the survival of the fittest, a lot of people we know must have been overlooked.
    (Grizzly Pete of Frozen Dog, alter ego of Col. William C. Hunter, who appears in Hunter's *Brass Tacks*, published in 1910.)

● **Groebe's Law.** The more complex the problem, the sooner the deadline.
    (Larry Groebe, San Antonio.)

● **Grosso's Second Law.** Education cannot be substituted for intelligence.
    (Gerald H. Grosso, Port Orchard, Wash.)

● **Gruber's Laws.** (1) Common sense and common knowledge are the two most uncommon things in the world. (2) Everybody has to be a somebody. (If not, why get up in the morning?) (3) If you can be intimidated, you will be.
    (John F. Gruber, Oak Creek, Wisc.)

● **Guinther's Law of Problem Solving.** It is better to solve problems than crises.

(John Guinther, in *The Malpractitioners,* Doubleday, 1978. *MBC.*)

● **Guinzburg's Warning.** If you ever find yourself quixotic enough to lie down with a vampire, don't be surprised if you get a love bite on your neck.

(Thomas Guinzburg, former president of Viking Press, after being ousted by its conglomerate owner. Quoted in Hillary Mills's "Publishing Notes," *The Washington Star,* May 13, 1979.)

● **Guppy Law.** When outrageous expenditures are divided finely enough, the public will not have enough stake in any one expenditure to squelch it.

(Fred Reed, columnist for *The Federal Times,* explaining how the bureaucracy minimizes popular resistance to a government program. *AO.*)

● **Gwen's Law.** Do not join encounter groups. If you enjoy being made to feel inadequate, call your mother.

(Liz Smith, from *The Mother Book,* Doubleday, 1978.)

H

- **Haber's Hypothesis.** For an employee, the number and length of coffee breaks varies directly with the amount of uncompleted work.

    (Meryl H. Haber, M.D., Professor and Chairman of the Department of Laboratory Medicine, University of Nevada, Reno. First published in *The Pathologist,* 1970.)

- **Hakala's Rule of Survival.** Pack your own parachute.
    (T. L. Hakala, Mesa, Ariz.)

- **Hall's Law of Return.** The nail that you drive flawlessly into a piece of wood without it buckling will be the same nail that you had previously singled out to show the salesperson how flimsy the nails are that he sold you.

    (John Hall, from William C. Callis, Falls Church, Va.)

- **Hall's Observations.** (1) The word *necessary* seldom is. (2) Most business decisions are based on one critical factor: which method will cause the least paperwork? *Janet's Corollary:* In government, the opposite is true.

    (Keith W. Hall, Harrisburg, Penn.)

- **Handel's Proverb.** You cannot produce a baby in one month by impregnating nine women!

    (Sally Handel, New York City.)

- **Hanson's Law of Progress.** Any new form is always longer and more complicated than the one it replaces.

    (Mark D. Hanson.)

● **Harris's Discoveries.** (1) Candy bars are smaller, but candy-bar wrappers are bigger. (2) A probable event is something good that ought to happen but doesn't. An unlikely event is something bad that should not happen but does. (3) If they catch you playing with a deck with more than four aces never admit you were cheating. Tell them you thought the game was canasta. (4) No one will ever say no to the question "You know what I mean?"

> (Roger Harris, Newark *Star-Ledger,* November 15, 1978.)

● **Harris's Law.** If a thing isn't worth doing, it isn't worth doing well.

> (Syndicated columnist Sydney J. Harris, whose father promulgated it as a cardinal rule of life. "I have made this a lifelong principle," says Harris, "and avoided dozens of onerous tasks.")

● **Hartka's Theorem.** You usually end up eating more cake after deciding to have only one thin piece than if you started with a bigger piece.

> (Thomas J. Hartka, Severna Park, Md. *Johns Hopkins Magazine,* May 1978.)

● **Harum's Theory of Fleas.** A moderate amount of fleas is good for a dog; it keeps him from broodin' on bein' a dog.

> (David Harum, the title character of E. N. Westcott's 1898 novel.)

● **Hasselbring's Law.** Never remember what you can afford to forget.

> (Andrew S. Hasselbring, Chillicothe, Ohio.)

● **Hassett's Third Law of Minutiae.** The intensity of interest in trivia is in reverse proportion to the magnitude of real-life problems encountered.

(W. Gilbert Hassett, Fairport, N.Y. This law came from his study of a retirement community where he found that the less people had to do, the fewer their real problems, the more they were concerned with little things. Why the Third Law of Minutiae? "The first two are inconsequential," says Hassett.)

● **Hazlitt's Observation.** The right thing to say always comes to mind after you've said the wrong thing and have no opportunity for rebuttal.
(John M. Hazlitt, South Bend, Ind.)

● **Health, Three Rules of.** One of the ancient natives has just confided to me a pearl of his ripe wisdom. Through 80 years of hard work, hard cider, strong tobacco, and simple food, he has only observed three rules of health, viz:
(1) Feet warm.
(2) Head cool.
(3) Bowels open.
(Richardson Wright, in *The Gardener's Bed Book,* J. B. Lippincott, 1929.)

● **Healy's Law of Distance.** The promised land always looks better from a distance.
(Pat Healy, reporter, *The Boston Globe. MBC.*)

● **Hebertson's Law of Budgets.** Don't be overly concerned with the cost of paper clips and other office supplies— fire people, and the paper clips will take care of themselves.
(David M. Hebertson, Sandy, Utah.)

● **Heifetz's Law.** No matter what you believe, you always find some people on your side that you wish were on the other side.
(Jascha Heifetz. From Earl M. Ryan, Birmingham, Mich.)

● **Hell's Angels Axiom.** When we do right you forget. When we do wrong you remember.

> (From Hunter Thompson's *The Hell's Angels*, Random House, 1967.)

● **Hellman's Product Development Rule.** If you drop something and it doesn't break, mark it heavy duty.

> (Mitch Hellman, Baltimore, learned while in new-product development.)

● **Hellrung's Law.** If you wait, it will go away. **Shavelson's Extension to Hellrung's Law.** . . . after having done its damage. **Grelb's Addition.** If it was bad, it will be back.

> (Loretta Hellrung, Alton, Mo. *EV.*)

● **Hempstone's Dictum.** When the federal cow wanders into the paddock, somebody's going to milk it.

> (Syndicated columnist Smith Hempstone, from his column of March 13, 1979.)

● **Henderson's Absolute.** There is nothing more cranky than a constipated gorilla.

> (Dr. J. Y. Henderson, chief veterinarian for Ringling Brothers and Barnum & Bailey Circus. Quoted in the *Los Angeles Times* by David Larsen.)

● **Hendrickson's Law.** If a problem causes too many meetings, the meetings eventually become more important than the problem.

> *(U/GT.)*

● **Henry's Law of Annual Reports.** The more rewrites a draft of an annual report is put through, the more the final, accepted draft for printing will match the original draft developed prior to administrative review.

(C. Henry Depew, Tallahassee, Fla. "Last year," he says, "the annual report I am responsible for producing . . . had thirteen partial and five full rewrites. The end draft . . . almost matched the initial draft.")

● **Herbst's Laws of Military Survival.** (1) Never annoy a finance clerk. Garbage in, garbage out. (2) Have a friend in personnel, finance, supply, the hospital, and the Orderly Room. It's not what you know but who you know. (3) So conduct yourself that when your name is mentioned in the Orderly Room, everyone says "Who?" The invisible man is never on the detail list. (4) There is no way you can get through a day without violating a regulation; therefore, choose the one nobody knows. A mob is the best camouflage. (5) As far as the military is concerned, a person's IQ is in direct ratio to his pay grade. There are more dumb airmen than dumb generals. (6) The detail list is always made the day before you put in for leave, and everyone who could replace you is going on leave the day of your detail. (7) Never assume anything. Thule AB Greenland is manned by the clowns who didn't read the small print. (8) You're never that "short" that someone wouldn't try to get your butt. Wait until you're out the gate before you tell them what you think of them. (9) Never listen to an officer who always says, "I was an enlisted man myself." If he knew what it was all about, he'd still be enlisted. (10) Crap seldom rolls uphill. It rolls down and spreads out.

(Anita M. Herbst, T. Sgt., USAF, San Antonio.)

● **Herman's Law.** Put your last change in a coffee machine or soft-drink dispenser, and have it run out of cups. Then watch the machine drink your coffee or soft drink.

(Michael P. Herman, Fox Point, Wisc.)

● **Herman's Rule.** If it works right the first time, you've obviously done something wrong.
(Pat [Mrs. Herman] Jett, Hillsboro, Mo.)

● **Herth's Law.** He who turns the other cheek too far gets it in the neck.
(U/Ra.)

● **Hickey's Law.** When one is looking at the bank clock for the temperature, the time will always show up.
(James K. Hickey, Washington, D.C.)

● **Highrise Golden Rule.** Do over Others as You Would Have Them Do over You—Remember One Person's Floor Is Another's Ceiling.
(U/Ra.)

● **Hildebrandt's Plotting Principle.** If you don't know where you are going, any road will get you there.
(John Hildebrandt, Market Research Specialist, Durham, N.C. From Gary Russell, New London, Minn.)

● **Hill's Pet Law.** The life expectancy of tropical fish is in direct, but opposite, proportion to their purchase price. *Corollary:* Expensive breeds of dogs always run away and get lost; mongrels never do.
(Pierre Allen Hill, York, Penn.)

● **Hinds's Observation.** Man is planned obsolescence.
(Alan Hinds, Marion, Ohio, who wrote shortly after throwing his back out of joint.)

● **Hoadley's Laws:** *Decision-making:* People will take tough decisions only when not taking them is tougher. *Inflation:* The roots of inflation are human. Everybody wants more for less work. The political response is axiomatic. It is more blessed to give than to receive, when it is somebody else's money.

> (Walter Hoadley, Executive Vice President and Chief Economist, Bank of America, at a seminar for senior executives, January 9, 1979. *TCA.*)

● **Hoffman's Law of Hilarity.** A true friend will not laugh at your joke until he retells it.

> (Henry R. Hoffman, Jr., Dallas.)

● **Hoffman's Rule of the Road.** After you have spent $375 to make sure your car is in top shape, invariably three cars will pass you on the turnpike and the drivers will sound their horns and point at your rear wheels.

> (Jon Hoffman. *MLS.*)

● **Holcombe's Law.** When everything appears to be going in one direction, take a long, hard look in the opposite direction.

> (Alfred D. Holcombe, Elmira, N.Y.)

● **Holistic Revelation.** In order to cover up a hole, you've got to dig a new one.

> *(U/Ra.)*

● **Hollander's Computing Laws.** (1) The most important data will be lost due to parity errors. (2) Two "standard" interfaces are about as similar as two snowflakes. (3) The program that never failed on your last computer will never run on your current computer.

> (Howard R. Hollander, Roy, Utah.)

● **Holloway's Rule.**

> It is impossible
>   to overestimate
> The unimportance
>   of practically everything.

(Clark Holloway, Pittsburgh, Penn.)

● **Holmes's Law.** Once you have eliminated the impossible, whatever remains, however improbable, must be the truth.
(Sherlock Holmes. *MLS.*)

● **Hooligan, Third Law of.** The ratio of south ends of northbound horses to the number of horses is always greater than one.
(Edward H. Seymour, New York City. *AO.*)

● **Horomorun Paradox.** The more one earns, the smaller becomes the proportion of one's salary one is allowed to spend.
(From *The Yam Factor,* by Martin Page, Doubleday, 1972.)

● **Horowitz's Laws.** (1) It is impossible to be a participant in the march of time and not get a few blisters. (2) There is hope for everything in nature except for the petrified forest.
(Stanley Horowitz, Flushing, N.Y.)

● **Horowitz's Rule.** A computer makes as many mistakes in two seconds as twenty men working twenty years.
(U/DRW.)

HOLMES'S LAW

● **Horton's Law.** For difficult Yes/No decisions (especially regarding the opposite sex) you'll always wish you did if you didn't, but you'll rarely wish you didn't if you did.

(Joseph A. Horton, M.D., Philadelphia, who adds that this is also known as "the Ah Posteriori Law.")

● **Hovancik's Wait till Tomorrow Principle.** Today is the last day of the first part of your life.

(John Hovancik. South Orange, N.J.)

Special Section 7

How to:

■ *Avoid Any Educational Problem (Applicable in Many Other Fields.)*
· Profess not to have *the* answer. This lets you out of having any answer.
· Say that we must not move too rapidly. This avoids the necessity of getting started.
· For every proposal set up an opposite and conclude that the "middle ground" (no motion whatever) represents the wisest course of action.
· Point out that any attempt to reach a conclusion is only a futile "quest for certainty." Doubt and uncertainty promote growth.
· When in a tight place say something that the group cannot understand.
· Say that the problem "cannot be separated" from other problems; therefore no problem can be solved until all other problems are solved.
· Point out that those who see the problem do so by virtue of personality traits; e.g. they are unhappy and transfer their dissatisfaction to the area under discussion.
· Ask what is meant by the question. When it is clarified there will be no time left for the answer.
· Retreat from the problem into endless discussion of various techniques for approaching it.
· Retreat into analogies and discuss them until everyone has forgotten the original problem.
· Point out that some of the greatest minds have struggled with the problem, implying that it does us credit to have thought of it.
· Be thankful for the problem. It has stimulated our best thinking

and has, therefore, contributed to our growth. It (the problem) should get a medal.

(From Mark Griesbach, Des Plaines, Ill., who credits it to "Dietrich, University of Chicago.")

■ *Differentiate Liberals from Conservatives.*

(1) Liberals want to solve the marijuana problem by making it legal. Conservatives want to solve the wife-beating problem by making it legal.

(2) Liberals want to continue the ban on prayer in the public schools, as they consider religion to be personal and private. They favor compulsory sex education. Conservatives want to ban sex education. They favor compulsory prayer.

(3) Liberals want to strike down the abortion laws, so that unwanted babies can be killed off before they are born. Conservatives want to strike down the welfare laws, so that unwanted babies can be starved to death after they are born.

(4) Conservatives want to outlaw pornography. Liberals want to outlaw handguns.

(5) The conservative would prevent rape by locking up his wife and daughters. The liberal would prevent rape by legalizing prostitution. Neither considers locking up rapists, because the liberal says it is society's fault and the conservative says it costs too much money.

(6) When it comes to equal rights for women, the conservative doesn't want to monkey with the Constitution. When it comes to a balanced federal budget, the liberal doesn't want to monkey with the Constitution.

(7) Conservatives curb their dogs. Liberals keep cats. They curb other people's dogs.

(The work of N. Sally Hass, Sleepy Hollow, Ill. She developed this scale when she discovered, "Many people think that liberals are permissive and conservatives are strict. Not so. Liberals are both permissive and strict. Conservatives are both permissive and strict. But they are permissive and strict about different things.")

■ *Learn to Write Goodly.*
(1) Don't use no double negatives.
(2) Make each pronoun agree with their antecedent.
(3) Join clauses good, like a conjunction should.
(4) About them sentence fragments.
(5) When dangling, watch your participles.
(6) Verbs has to agree with their subject.
(7) Just between you and I, case is important to.
(8) Don't write run-on sentences they are hard to read.
(9) Don't use commas, which aren't necessary.
(10) Try to not oversplit infinitives.
(11) It is important to use your apostrophe's correctly.
(12) Proofread your writing to if any words out.
(13) Correct spelling is esential.
     (From the newsletter of the Naval Supply Systems Command, *What's SUP.*)

■ *Name Things Impressively.*
I. General Purpose Argot Generator.
When in need of an authoritative phrase for a concept, project, or whatever, pull a three-digit number out of the air and select the corresponding words from the three columns. The number 982, for example, yields "Balanced Third-Generation Flexibility."

A	B	C
(0) Integrated	Management	Options
(1) Total	Organizational	Flexibility
(2) Systematized	Monitored	Capability
(3) Parallel	Reciprocal	Mobility
(4) Functional	Digital	Programming
(5) Responsive	Logistical	Concept
(6) Optional	Transitional	Time Phase

(7) Synchronized	Incremental	Projection
(8) Compatible	Third-Generation	Hardware
(9) Balanced	Policy	Contingency

(This guide to impressive but fuzzy words is known by a number of names including "The Baffle-Gab Thesaurus," "The Buzz Phrase Projector," and "The Handy Obfuscator." It has been widely mimeographed, photocopied, and published in trade magazines. It reputedly came out of some office of the Royal Canadian Air Force and was popularized in Washington by Philip Broughton, an HEW official.)

II. Medical Argot Generator.

Like the previous generator, this device requires random three-digit numbers. The only difference is that the user is to fill in column B with the accepted buzz words of the specialty or sub-specialty that he or she is involved in.

A	B	C
(1) Diagnostic	_____	Prevention
(2) Chronic	_____	Screening
(3) Systematic	_____	Evaluation
(4) Limited access	_____	Management
(5) Clinical	_____	Follow-up
(6) Ancillary	_____	Outreach
(7) Therapeutic	_____	Placebo
(8) Prospective	_____	Service pattern
(9) Retrospect	_____	Encounter
(10) Prognostic	_____	Incidence
(11) Preventive	_____	Intervention
(12) Life-threatening	_____	Trauma

(Writer John Paul Kowal, *Medical Dimensions,* December 1977.)

● **Howard's First Law of Theater.** Use it.
(U/GT.)

● **Howe's Verities.** (1) When you're in trouble, people who call to sympathize are really looking for the particulars. (2) When in doubt in society, shake hands. (3) Everyone hates a martyr; it's no wonder martyrs were burned at the stake. (4) A good many of your tragedies probably look like comedies to others. (5) Put cream and sugar on a fly, and it tastes very much like a black raspberry. (6) Families with babies, and families without babies, are so sorry for each other. (6) Where the guests at a gathering are well acquainted, they eat 20 percent more than they otherwise would.
(E. W. Howe, from his *Country Town Sayings* [1911].)

● **Hubbard's Credos.** (1) If a man says to you, "It isn't the money; it's the principle of the thing," I'll lay you six to one it's the money. (2) The fellow who owns his own home is always just coming out of the hardware store. (3) Everything comes to him who waits, except a loaned book. (4) There is somebody at every dinner party who eats all the celery.
("Kin" Hubbard, humorist and cartoonist, from various sources.)

● **Huffmann's Reminder.** Remember, it's everywhere.
(William Huffmann, from Martin E. Shotzberger, Arlington, Va.)

● **Huguelet's Law of Systems Design.** Frozen specifications are like the abominable snowman, both are myths and both melt with the slightest application of heat.
(Thomas V. Huguelet, President, Huguelet Systems Corp., Chicago.)

● **Huhn's Law.** You're not late until you get there.
(U/Ra.)

● **Human Ecology, The Three Laws of.** (1) There is no such thing as an independent individual, no such invention as an isolated technology, no such thing as a single resource, and no such place as an independent nation-state. (2) Humankind is an organized ecosystem of flows and stocks of transformed and reconstructed materials, money, energy, and information. (3) One generation's, community's, or culture's answers, solutions, or opportunities become other people's problems.
> (From Don G. Miles, the Feeding People Programme Fund, Australia.)

● **Hunter's Rule.** You see a lot when you haven't got your gun.
(U/Ra.)

● **Huster's Law.** Software "bugs" are always infectious.
> (Dwight A. Huster, State College, Penn.)

● **Hutzler's Refutation.** Desperation, not necessity, is the Mother of Invention.
> (Thomas L. Hutzler, T. Sgt., USAF, Fort Fisher, N.C.)

● **Iannuzzi's Universal Law of Justice.** Truth is trouble.
(*U/* From a column in *Car and Driver* by Patrick Bedard.)

● **Ike Tautology, The.** Things are more like they are now than they have ever been before.
(Dwight D. Eisenhower. From Paul Martin to *DRW.*)

● **Inch, Law of.** In designing any type of construction, no overall dimension can be totaled correctly after 4:30 P.M. on Friday. *Corollary 1:* Under the same conditions, if any minor dimensions are given to 1/16 of an inch, they cannot be totaled at all. *Corollary 2:* The correct total will become self-evident at 8:15 A.M. on Monday.
(From an unsigned list of laws brought to the Center's attention by Ray Boston.)

● **Inge's Natural Law.** The whole of nature is a conjunction of the verb to eat, in the active and passive.
(Nineteenth-century clergyman/writer William Ralph Inge.)

● **Institutional Input, Law of.** The wider the inter-departmental consultation on a problem, the less will any agency accept responsibility for the final report.
(*The Washington Star* editorial, February 18, 1979.)

● **Institutions, Law of.** The opulence of the front-office decor varies inversely with the fundamental solvency of the firm.
(*U/DRW.*)

● **Intelligence, Laws of.** (1) Intelligence is simple; all you have to do is find the needle in the haystack. (2) Don't forget to recognize the needle when you see it.

(Gen. William Davidson, head of the Office of Strategic Services [OSS] during World War II, to *TCA.*)

● **Inverse Peter Principle.** Everyone rises to his own level of indispensability, and gets stuck there.

(Dr. Barry Boehm, TRW, during a speech before the Special Interest Group on Aerospace Computing, March 19, 1979. *RS.*)

● **Iron Law of Consulting.** If I make the decision and I am right, you will never remember. If I make the decision and I am wrong, you will never *forget.*

(From *Operations Research for Immediate Application: A Quick and Dirty Manual* by Robert E. D. Woolsey and Huntington S. Swanson, Harper & Row, 1975. *RS.*)

Special Section 8

Irregular Verbs.

I am firm; You are obstinate; He is a pig-headed fool.

I am an epicure; You are a gourmand; He has both feet in the trough.

I am sparkling; You are unusually talkative; He is drunk.

I am farseeing; You are a visionary; He's a fuzzy-minded dreamer.

I am beautiful; You have quite good features; She isn't bad-looking, if you like that type.

I have reconsidered; You have changed your mind; He has gone back on his word.

I dream; You escape; He needs help.

I am at my prime; You are middle-aged; He's getting old.

I am a liberal; You are a radical; He is a communist.

I am casual; You are informal; He is an unshaven slob.

I am in charge of public relations; You exaggerate; He misleads.

I am a camera; You are a copycat; He is a plagiarist.

I am righteously indignant; You are annoyed; He is making a fuss about nothing.

I am a behavioral researcher; You are curious about people; He is a Peeping Tom.

I am nostalgic; You are old-fashioned; He is living in the past.

(The game of "Irregular Verbs" or "Conjugations" was created quite a few years ago by philosopher Bertrand Russell on the BBC program *Brains Trust* when he declined "I am firm," the first example on our list. Ever since, people have been discovering new examples of how we approach self, present company, and those beyond earshot. The examples used here have come from a number of sources including *The New Statesman, The Nation, Harper's, Time, Isaac Asimov's Treasury of Humor,* Houghton Mifflin, 1971, and Ralph L. Woods's *How to Torture Your Mind,* Funk & Wagnalls, 1969.)

● **Irreversible Law of the Toe Holes.** No matter which side of the toe of the sock a hole is in, you will always put the sock on so that your big toe protrudes through the hole.

(Tom Eddins, Harding University, Searcy, Ark.)

● **Irving's Inquiry.** Who ever hears of fat men heading a riot?

(Washington Irving.)

● **Isaac's Law of Public Transportation.** No matter which direction you are going, the bus/streetcar going in the other direction will come first. *Corollary:* If you are in a hurry, at least three buses/streetcars going in the other direction will come first. (Richard Isaac, M.D., Toronto.)

J

- **Jackson's Economic Discovery.** If a young man or woman goes to any state university in this country for four years, it will cost less than $20,000. But if he or she goes to the state penitentiary for four years, it will cost slightly more than $50,000.
  (Jesse Jackson, quoted in *Newsweek,* July 10, 1978.)

- **Jackson's Food Physics Laws.** (1) When stale, things innately crisp will become soft and things innately soft will become crisp. (2) The temperature of liquids gravitates toward room temperature, at which those drinks served hot are too cool and those served cold are too warm.
  (Julie S. Jackson, Laurel, Md.)

- **Jackson's Laws.** (1) The next war can't start until the generals from the previous one have had time to write their memoirs. (2) Shopping centers are for people who don't have to go to the bathroom. (3) Baseball players must spit when the TV camera closes in on them.
  (Michael Jackson, KABC Radio, Los Angeles.)

- **Jackson's Observation on Fame.** Fans don't boo nobodies.
  (Reggie Jackson.)

- **Jacob's Laws of Organization.** (1) Never put anything away temporarily. (A dish that is taken in from the dining room and put on the sink, instead of directly into the dishwasher, ends up being put away twice.) (2) Take pity on your poor biographer (. . . organize and date your diaries and albums). (3) Why are people always complaining about being behind when all you have to do to keep up is a little every day? (4) Throwing things away is as great a joy as acquiring things. (5) If it's worth going, there's something worth taking with you. (6) If you are no good at this, give up—and cherish the nearest organized person.

(From Judith Martin's article "Organized!" in the Weekend section of *The Washington Post,* December 29, 1978. Jacob Perlman was her father.)

● **Jane's Gospel.** When there are two or more identical articles to be built or repaired, difficulty will be encountered, but only while attempting to build or repair the second (or last) one. *Corollary 1:* When both the hot and cold water faucets are leaking, the knob of the first one will be removed, the washer replaced, and the knob put back on with no complications. While attempting to repair the second, however, one will encounter (a) a permanently welded knob, (b) a screw-head stripped bare, (c) a knob that fit until removed but cannot possibly be reused, or (d) all of the above. *Corollary 2:* If the first article is dismantled again in order to determine why it went back together so easily, it will not.

(Jane L. Hassler, Marina del Rey, Cal.)

● **Jefferson's Ten Commandments.** (1) Never put off till tomorrow what you can do today. (2) Never trouble another for what you can do yourself. (3) Never spend your money before you have earned it. (4) Never buy what you don't want because it is cheap. (5) Pride costs more than hunger, thirst, and cold. (6) We seldom report of having eaten too little. (7) Nothing is troublesome that we do willingly. (8) How much pain evils cost us that have never happened! (9) Take things always by the smooth handle. (10) When angry, count to ten before you speak; if very angry, count to a hundred.

(Thomas Jefferson. Found in B. C. Forbes [ed.] *Thoughts on the Business Life* [1937].)

● **Jenkins's Rules for Football Betting.** (1) Never take a tip from a guy eating in a luncheonette. . . . (2) Find a team whose players' wives have an abundance of mink coats. Wait until the mink coats are favored by ten or more against a team playing under .500, then load up on the dog. The dog could win the whole game. (3) A team with too many members in the Fellowship of Christian Athletes can draw up to three delay penalties a game. Too much praying in the huddle. (4) Go with a good passing team against defensive backs who collect art. (5) A team with its entire offensive line living within a block of a drugstore could go all the way. (6) Finally, keep an eye out for the Ivy Leaguer in a key position if the Dow takes a sudden dip.

>   (Dan Jenkins, adapted from his his article "Getting in on a Zurich," in *Sports Illustrated.*)

● **Jesuit Principle.** It is better to ask for forgiveness than permission.

>   (Richard Molony.)

● **Jigsaw's Searching Conclusion.** You are standing on the piece that has to go in next.

>   (Elizabeth W. Jefferson, Roanoke, Va.)

● **Jinny's Second Law.** At a party, if you run out of ice, the guests stand around and bitch; if you run out of liquor, they go home.

>   (Virginia W. Smith, who is *MLS*'s mother.)

● **Jinny's Sister's Legacy.** Be careful what you give people as gifts; you may get it back when they die.

>   (Margaret W. Carpenter. *MLS.*)

● **Joachim's Explanation.** Nonsmokers create a vacuum and draw the smoke toward themselves.

>   (Gary Joachim, a smoker, who told it to Dianne Coates, a nonsmoker from Reseda, Cal.)

Special Section 9

Job Performance Evaluation.
(The Center has received half a dozen variations on this important personnel rating system—all unattributed. This particular version was sent by *ME. FSP* collected the next item.)

Performance Level

Performance Factor	Outstanding	High Satisfactory
Quality	Leaps tall buildings with a single bound.	Needs running start to jump tall buildings.
Timeliness	Is faster than a speeding bullet.	Only as fast as a speeding bullet.
Initiative	Is stronger than a locomotive.	Is stronger than a bull elephant.
Adaptability	Walks on water consistently.	Walks on water in emergencies.
Communication	Talks with God.	Talks with the angels.
Relationship	Belongs in general management.	Belongs in executive ranks.
Planning	Too bright to worry.	Worries about future.

Satisfactory	Low Satisfactory	Unsatisfactory
Can only leap small buildings.	Crashes into buildings.	Cannot recognize buildings.
Somewhat slower than a bullet.	Can only shoot bullets.	Wounds self with bullets.
Is stronger than a bull.	Shoots the bull.	Smells like a bull.
Washes with water.	Drinks water.	Passes water in emergencies.
Talks to himself.	Argues with himself.	Loses those arguments.
Belongs in rank and file.	Belongs behind a broom.	Belongs with competitor.
Worries about present.	Worries about past.	Too dumb to worry.

Job Performance, What the Descriptions Mean. The military uses fitness reports in the evaluation of personnel performance. The following comes from the U.S. Navy but applies to general use.

Average: Not too bright.

Exceptionally well qualified: Has committed no major blunders to date.

Active socially: Drinks heavily.

Zealous attitude: Opinionated.

Character above reproach: Still one step ahead of the law.

Unlimited potential: Will stick until retirement.

Quick thinking: Offers plausible excuses for errors.

Takes pride in his work: Conceited.

Takes advantage of every opportunity to progress: Buys drinks for superiors.

Forceful and aggressive: Argumentative.

Indifferent to instruction: Knows more than his seniors.

Stern disciplinarian: A bastard.

Tactful in dealing with superiors: Knows when to keep his mouth shut.

Approaches difficult problems with logic: Finds someone else to do the job.

A keen analyst: Thoroughly confused.

Not a "desk" man: Did not go to college.

Expresses himself well: Speaks English.

Spends extra hours on job: Miserable home life.

Conscientious and careful: Scared.

Meticulous in attention to detail: A nitpicker.

Demonstrates qualities of leadership: Has a loud voice.

Judgment is usually sound: Lucky.

Maintains professional attitude: A snob.

Keen sense of humor: Has a vast repertory of dirty jokes.

Strong adherence to principles: Stubborn.

Gets along extremely well with superiors and subordinates alike: A coward.

NOT A "DESK" MAN

Slightly below average: Stupid.
Of great value to the organization: Turns work in on time.

● **Joe Cooch's Law.** (1) If things are military and make sense, coincidence has entered the picture. (2) To hell with the content, let's get the format straight. (3) Personnel officers exist primarily for the purpose of screwing up other people's careers. (4) The most complicated problems always arise at the most remote locations. (5) Writing a directive and getting people to pay attention to it are two entirely different operations. (6) Staff studies should always be written in support of foregone conclusions; assumptions will be furnished later. (7) The more esoteric the presentation, the thicker the accent of the person presenting it. (8) Generals must be kept busy or their subordinates will be. (9) Greatest consideration in personnel matters is given to those individuals who are the least efficient and the most troublesome; or, if you want top-level support, screw up. (10) It is illegal for any headquarters to admit error. (11) Planners are people who take implausible assumptions, apply these to conditions that could not possibly exist, using resources that will undoubtedly not be available, to produce a plan of action that is inconceivable to be followed out. (12) One thousand guesses added together are not necessarily more accurate than one big guess. (13) The longer you work on a casualty estimate, the less accurate it becomes. (14) If people don't obey a Regulation, write another more complicated. (15) Invariably, the least knowledgeable of individuals is the most vocal.

(We don't know who Joe Cooch is and wonder aloud if he might be a new incarnation of Murphy—or, at least, a figure created in Murphy's image. Whatever, his wisdom in the form of the multipart "Cooch's Law" is starting to show up with Murphy-like frequency. Examples of adaptations of Joe Cooch's code to fields outside the military [scientific research, for one] are beginning to appear. Our guess is that Joe Cooch is on his way to household-name status. Timothy J. Rolfe of the University of Chicago was the first to bring the Cooch contribution to the attention of the Center.)

● **Johns Hopkins Miraculous Secret for the Early Recovery of Patients, The.** Inflation.
(*U*/ Nurse/*Ra.*)

● **Johnson's Creative Caveat.** No man but a blockhead ever wrote except for money.
(Samuel Johnson.)

● **Johnson's Law of Indices.** Any subject, no matter how abstruse or unlikely, will be found in an index, except the subject for which you are searching, no matter how common or likely.
(Rita Johnson, Stanley, N.D.)

● **Jones's Law of Authority.** The importance of an authority figure in a field is inversely proportional to the amount that is known about the subject.
(Don Jones, from James S. Benton, Los Angeles. The same Don Jones is responsible for the next set of laws.)

● **Jones's Laws of Innovation and the Organization.** (1) Organizational strength increases with time. (2) Innovative capacity is inversely proportional to organizational strength. *Corollary 1:* The least likely organization to make a significant improvement in a concept is the one that developed it. *Corollary 2:* The first step in developing a new concept is to bypass the existing organization. *Corollary 3:* Organizing for innovation is a contradiction in terms.

● **Jones's Mathematical Law.** Twice nothing is still nothing.
(Cyrano Jones, *Star Trek,* "The Trouble with Tribbles." *JS.*)

● **Jones's Rule of the Road.** The easiest way to refold a road map is differently.
(Franklin P. Jones, in *The Wall Street Journal.*)

● **Jones's Static Principle.** In a static organization, one accedes to his level of comfort.
(From J. Thomas Parry, Rockford, Ill., who attributes it to

Hugh Jones, manager of the Minneapolis *TV Guide* office. Parry says, "Mr. Jones, having been in an unchanging job for many years, developed this corollary to the Peter Principle.")

● **Jones's 3:00 A.M. Theory.** Truly important information should be retained and ready even if the boss calls at 3:00 A.M. and wakes you from a deep sleep.
(Kenneth J. Jones, Hunt Valley, Md.)

● **Jordan's Laws.** *Of Survival:* You can get over anything but a gravel in your shoe. *Of Technology:* Invention is the mother of necessity. (How long did mankind get along satisfactorily without the telephone?) *Of Psychiatry:* The client already knows all the answers, but he won't tell. The psychiatrist is lucky to guess the right questions.
(D. Wylie Jordan, M.D., Austin, Tex.)

● **Juall's Law on Nice Guys.** Nice guys don't always finish last: (a) Sometimes they don't finish. (b) Sometimes they don't get a chance to start.
(Wally Juall, East Lansing, Mich.)

● **Juhani's Law.** The compromise will always be more expensive than either of the suggestions it's compromising.
(U/DRW.)

● **Juliet's Advice.** (1) Never start before you are ready. (2) People will do to you what you let them.
(Juliet Awon-Uibopuu, River Edge, N.J.)

K

● **Kagan's Principle of Operational Verisimilitude.** You don't test something to see if it will work if you think it won't work.

>(Susan Kagan, from Shel Kagan, New York City.)

● **Kagle's Rule for Winning Stock Car Races.** Keep to the left, and get back here as soon as you can.

>(Reds Kagle, late-model sportsman champion, Old Dominion Speedway, 1976–77, Manassas, Va. *JCG.*)

● **"Kamoose" Taylor's Hotel Rules and Regulations.** (A selection.)

A deposit must be made before towels, soap, or candles can be carried to rooms. When boarders are leaving, a rebate will be made on all candles or parts of candles not burned or eaten.

Not more than one dog allowed to be kept in each single room.

Quarrelsome or boisterous persons, also those who shoot off without provocation guns or other explosive weapons on the premises, and all boarders who get killed, will not be allowed to remain in the House.

When guests find themselves or their baggage thrown over the fence, they may consider that they have received notice to quit.

The proprietor will not be accountable for anything.

Only regularly registered guests will be allowed the special privilege of sleeping on the Bar Room floor.

Meals served in own rooms will not be guaranteed in any way. Our waiters are hungry and not above temptation.

All guests are requested to rise at 6:00 A.M. This is imperative as the sheets are needed for tablecloths.

To attract attention of waiters or bellboys, shoot a hole through the door panel. Two for ice water, three shots for a deck of cards, and so on.

(Rules posted September 1, 1882, at the MacLeod Hotel in Alberta by Henry "Kamoose" Taylor, proprietor. This important piece of Canadian lore appears in *Columbo's Little Book of Canadian Proverbs, Graffiti, Limericks and Other Vital Matters* by John Robert Columbo, Hurtig Publishing, 1975.)

● **Kaplan's Dictum.** If you are unable to decide between two things, do whichever is cheapest.

(*U*/Fred Bondy, Wilmette, Ill.)

● **Karni's Law of Telephones.** The cessation of ringing of a phone is *not* a function of the responder's distance, velocity, or time of access. (It will stop ringing just when you reach for it, no matter how far you have to come, how fast—or slowly—you have traveled to cover the distance between you and said phone.)

(S. Karni, Professor, University of New Mexico, Department of Electrical Engineering and Computer Science. Karni supports his discovery with this statement: "[It] is truly empirical, having been tested in the field for over twenty years [a total of some 40,000 experiments]. No theoretical proof is known to exist at this time, although some of the best brains are involved in its pursuit.")

● **Kass's Truth.** If you plan a pot luck for a club of thirty-seven members, you will end up with a meal of thirty-seven jars of dill pickles.

(Connie Kass, St. Paul.)

● **Kathleen's Hypothesis of Earth-Water Kinesis.** The lighter the color, the higher the heel, and the more the cost of the

shoes, the deeper the mud in the puddle just outside the car door.
(Kathleen, known to Michael L. Lazare, Armonk, N.Y.)

● **Katz's Laws.** (1) No new theory is recognized until some expert claims it was plagiarized. (2) Never send your new theorem to a specialist in counterexamples.
(Robert Katz, Rockport, Mass.)

● **Kaufman's Laws.** (1) A policy is a restrictive document to prevent a recurrence of a single incident, in which that incident is never mentioned. (2) A roadblock is a negative reaction, based on irrelevant assumption.
(J. Jerry Kaufman, Dallas.)

● **Kaul's Collection.** (1) It does not rain on water-resistant materials. (2) The only thing alike in all cultures is the police. (3) A sinking ship gathers no moss. (4) Abstinence makes the heart grow fonder. (5) Do not try to solve all life's problems at once —learn to dread each day as it comes. (6) Crime doesn't pay unless you write a book about it. (7) A fool and his money are welcomed everywhere. (8) Don't bake cookies; the children will only eat them. (9) A man can have more money than brains, but not for long. (10) Suicide is the sincerest form of self-criticism. (11) A coward dies a thousand deaths, a hero dies but one—but which one?
(Donald Kaul, *The Des Moines Register.* These are laws and observations sent to Kaul by readers of his "Over the Coffee" column.)

● **Kautzmann's Law of Negativism.** Whatever you propose to do can't be done. *Corollary:* If they do what you propose, it won't work.
(Gary E. Kautzmann, Allentown, Penn.)

● **Kaye's Duplicate Bridge Players' Rule of Thumb.** The

laws of chance positively ensure that you will always play the most difficult contracts against the most competent opponents, and the "laydowns" against the beginners. *Corollary:* Whenever a partnership has lost a match by a very few points, each partner will invariably remember (and be willing to discuss ad nauseam) his own brilliant plays and his partner's errors.

(Joan C. Kaye, Los Gatos, Cal.)

● **Keller's Law of the Theater.** A whisper backstage will be heard with greater intensity than a line spoken in a normal voice on stage.

(William S. Keller, Streamwood, Ill.)

● **Kellough's Laws of Waiting.** (1) The amount of time you must wait is directly proportional to the uncomfortableness of the settings you must wait in. (2) The magazines in a doctor's, dentist's, or barber's place of business are always at least three months old. The boringness of those magazines is directly proportional to the length of time you have to wait.

(David Kellough, Chillicothe, Ohio.)

● **Kelly's Run-Around Theorem.** (1) To get published, one should get a literary agent. (2) To get a literary agent, one should be published.

(William W. Kelly, Hollywood, Fla.)

● **Kener's Law.** Tape doesn't stick where (or when) you want it. Tape only sticks to itself.

(Reed Kener, from Larry Groebe, San Antonio.)

● **Keokuk, First Law of.** The ability and adeptness of the towboat captain varies inversely with the rapidity of the approach of 8:30 A.M. and 4:30 P.M.

(Constance E. Campbell, Keokuk, Iowa. She explains: "Keokuk . . . is a river town on the Mississippi River.

There is a swing-span toll bridge connecting Keokuk and Hamilton, Illinois, at the foot of Main Street. . . . The times a new, inexperienced towboat captain seems always to be trying unsuccessfully to maneuver his towboat into our lock is invariably the times people are trying to get to work, or to get home from work.'')

● **Kerouac's Admonition.** Walking on water wasn't built in a day.

(Jack Kerouac.)

● **Kerr's Three Rules for a Successful College.** Have plenty of football for the alumni, sex for the students, and parking for the faculty.

(Clark Kerr. *MLS.*)

● **Key to Happiness.** You may speak of love and tenderness and passion, but real ecstasy is discovering you haven't lost your keys after all.

(U/Ra.)

● **Khomeini Corollary.** Take the revolution to where the reporters want to be and you'll get worldwide coverage.

(Charles Peters, in *The Washington Monthly.* Peters says that this discovery is owed to the Shah of Iran, who landed the Ayatollah Khomeini in Paris. "Now reporters who would never dream of going to Meshed, Tabriz, or Zahidan could cover the main issues of the Iranian revolution from Paris.'')

● **King's Religious Observation.** The shorter the gospel, the longer the sermon.

(Donald King, Philadelphia.)

● **Klawans-Rinsley Law.** Large projects require more time, small projects require less time.

(Alan J. Klawans and Donald B. Rinsley, M.D.)

● **Kneass's Law.** If you are a writer, editor, publisher, or affiliated with an advertising agency, everyone knows more about your business than you do.

(Jack Kneass, Huntington Beach, Cal.)

● **Knowles's Law.** The length of debate is in inverse proportion to the importance of the subject.

(Robert P. Knowles, New Richmond, Wisc., twenty-two-year veteran of the state legislature. He writes, "At one point the Wisconsin Senate spent an entire day debating the proper construction of a doghouse. The bill finally failed to pass. The next day a highly complex bill having to do with a three-phase formula for corporate taxation passed without a word of debate or a dissenting vote.")

● **Knowlton's Law of Involvement.** Fight to the death for anything in which you truly believe—but keep those kinds of commitments to a bare minimum.

(Gary Knowlton, Portland, Ore.)

● **Koolman's Laws of Physics.** [As expounded to an unfortunate student over several years by many professors, based on the original premise learned in high school: PHYSICS IS AN EXACT SCIENCE.]

(1) If it gives you trouble, get rid of it. If you can't get rid of it, ignore it.

(2) If you can't understand it, it is intuitively obvious.

Corollary: If it works, use it.

(3) Occam's razor is invalid (and dull).

Corollary: If you think it's confusing now, wait till you find out what it's really about.

Corollary: Logical constructs are only used to make the picture of the universe more confusing than before.

Corollary: Use generalities wherever possible, as it makes things more difficult to understand.

Corollary: Always introduce an arbitrary constant to confuse the issue.

(4) All fundamental particles (constants, rules, etc.) of the same kind are identical, except those that are different.

Corollary: Anything that breaks a general rule is either totally correct and the rule wrong, or is to be ignored.

(5) A meaningful concept is one that violates every rule possible.

Corollary: A meaningful concept is usually meaningless and confusing, unless your instructor or boss formulated it, in which case you'd best learn it anyway.

(6) A physicist cannot relate to his environment.

Corollary: If you want to prove something, remake the universe so that it is true.

(7) All inconsistencies are consistent with recognized theories.

(8) Contradiction is the essence of all physical theorems.

(9) In any calculation, a constant of "π," "e," or "-1" is always lost.

(10) Always use ideal constructs with no real analogues to explain them.

Corollary: Everything is useless.

Corollary: Reality doesn't work.

Corollary: If you prove it can't exist, it does, and vice versa.

Corollary: See *Law 6.*

(Ron Koolman, Cincinnati, Ohio.)

● **Korzybski's Warning.** God may forgive you your sins, but your nervous system won't.

(Alfred Korzybski, scientist and writer. *ME.*)

● **Kottmeyer's Ring-Around-the-Tub Principle.** Telephones displace bodies immersed in water.

(Martin S. Kottmeyer, Carlyle, Ill.)

● **Krafft's Scale of Dumb (a.k.a. The Seven Deadly Dumbs).** [Created for military application but may be tailored to fit the particular needs of any type of organization or endeavor by removing and substituting the italicized words.]

Adjectival	Category	Application
Gross Dumb	1	Common dumb, frequently found at *squad or platoon level.*
Public Dumb	2	Less common than a gross dumb; frequently seen amongst the leadership at *company level.*
Gross Public Dumb	3	The all-emcompassing "combination of ingredients" dumb.
Incredible Dumb	4	Also known as "aggravated dumb." Causes the *Post Commander* to sit up and take notice. May have visibility at *higher headquarters.*
Congenital Dumb	5	Encountered most frequently in *other units.* We all know folks like this, but Category 5's can be excused with, "It ain't their fault—they were born that way."

Contagious Dumb	6	Frequent and prolonged exposure to *certain staff officers at the installation* causes this. Incubation period: 24 to 30 months. Temporary relief of symptoms by avoiding all staff meetings and *hot-line calls.*
Terminal Dumb	7	What happens to a victim of contagious dumb unless the condition is treated immediately.

(Maj. Gary R. Krafft, U.S. Army, Fort Meade, Md.)

● **Kramer's Law of Ploygraphy.** Whenever someone says he is being perfectly frank, he is being less than perfectly frank.
(Victor H. Kramer, from Andrew Jay Schwartzman, Washington, D.C.)

● **Krause's Discovery.** In the jungle, a press card is just another piece of paper.
(Charles Krause, *The Washington Post.*)

● **Krupka's Observation.** When you see an individual wearing a white lab coat, you can be sure he thinks he is a scientist.
(U/From an unpublished paper, "Famous Laws and Principles of Science," by Ray S. Hansen, Corvallis, Ore., and Robert A. Sweeney, Buffalo.)

● **Krutch's Indictment.** The most serious charge that can be brought against New England is not Puritanism but February. (Naturalist Joseph Wood Krutch.)

L

● **Lada's Commuter Corollary.** As soon as construction is complete on the fastest, most convenient expressway route from your home to your place of work, you will be transferred to another place of work.

(Stephen C. Lada, Detroit.)

● **Landers's Law of the Pinch.** Usually when the shoe fits —it's out of style.

(Ann Landers, in her column for February 6, 1977.)

● **Landon's Law of Politics.** It's a sin in politics to land a soft punch.

(Alf Landon, in an interview with David Broder, *The Washington Post,* December 14, 1977.)

● **Lansburgh's Observation.** There's no column on the scorecard headed "remarks."

(Sidney Lansburgh, Jr., quoted in Julius M. Westheimer's column in *The Baltimore Evening Sun,* March 22, 1979.)

● **Larson's Conclusion.** Shunning women, liquor, gambling, smoking, and eating will not make one live longer. It will only seem like it.

(M. Sgt. Robert V. Larson, USAF [retired], Golden Valley, Minn.)

● **Latecomer's Rule.** If you are impatiently waiting for someone to arrive who is late, go to the bathroom and that person will arrive instantly in your absence.

(A. S. Boccuti, Baltimore.)

● **Laur's Advice to Negotiators and Traders.** You've got to let the monkey *have* the banana every once in a while.
(Ed Laur, Amarillo, Tex.)

● **Laura's Law.** No child throws up in the bathroom.
(U/DRW.)

● **Law Laws.** (1) Aphorism is better than none. (2) In the beginning Murphy condensed the human condition into twelve laws. The rest of us want to get into somebody's book.
(Ryan Anthony, Tucson.)

● **Lawrence's Laws.** (1) Paperwork is inversely proportional to useful work. (2) In any bureaucracy, the triviality of any position can be derived by counting the number of administrative assistants.
(Bob Ackley, T. Sgt., USAF, Plattsmouth, Neb.)

Special Section 10

Lawyer's Language. Toward a better understanding of the law . . .

"As Your Honor Well Recalls." Tip-off by a lawyer that he is about to refer to a long-forgotten or imaginary case. (Adapted from a similar definition by Miles Kington, *Punch,* November 12, 1975.)
Basic Concept. Murder—don't do it; Theft—don't do it; Fraud —don't do it; etc. (G. Guy Smith, Media, Penn.)

Brief. Long and windy document. Should be at least 10,000 words long to qualify.

Costs. Amount required to bankrupt the acquitted. (Miles Kington.)

Duty of the Lawyer. When there is a rift in the lute, the business of the lawyer is to widen the rift and gather the loot. (Arthur Garfield Hays.)

Equality Under the Law. ". . . forbids the rich as well as the poor to sleep under bridges, to beg in the streets, and to steal bread." (Anatole France.)

Incongruous. Where our laws are made. (Bennett Cerf.)

"It has been long known that . . ." "I haven't been able to find the original reference."

"It might be argued that . . ." "I have such a good answer for this argument that I want to make sure it is raised."

Lex Clio Volente. The client is always right—particularly when he has further causes to entrust. (Del Goldsmith, *American Bar Association Journal.*)

Nine Points of the Law, The. (1) A good deal of money. (2) A good deal of patience. (3) A good case. (4) A good lawyer. (5) A good counsel. (6) Good witnesses. (7) A good jury. (8) A good judge. (9) Good luck.

Proper Pronoun. Louis Nizer has pointed out that most lawyers on winning a case will say, "We have won," but when justice frowns on the case the lawyer customarily remarks, "You have lost."

Plea Bargaining. Ending a sentence with a proposition.

Res Ipsa Loquitur. Latin for "the thing speaks for itself." Anything that speaks for itself is an abomination to the law and reason enough for a lawyer to be paid to speak for something that speaks for itself. (Adapted from Miles Kington.)

Will. Where there's a will, there's a lawsuit. (Oliver Herford.)

"With All Due Respect." Introductory phrase for a disrespectful statement.

"Yes, Your Honor." Witty rejoinder by lawyer to judge. (Miles Kington.)

● **LAX Law.** Flying is not in itself dangerous, but the air is like the sea, very unforgiving of those who make mistakes.
(Sign seen in a hangar at the Los Angeles International Airport. William C. Young, Ballston Lake, N.Y.)

● **Le Bon's Mot.** Science has promised us truth. It has never promised us either peace or happiness.
(Gustave Le Bon.)

● **Le Carré's Assumption.** When in doubt about something like this, assume a screw-up.
(John le Carré, quoted in the *Los Angeles Times,* April 8, 1974. *RS.*)

● **Lec's Immutables.** (1) The first requisite for immortality is death. (2) All gods were immortal. (3) Even a flounder takes sides.
(Stanislaw J. Lec, from *Unkempt Thoughts,* St. Martin's Press, 1962.)

● **Lee's Law.** Mother said there would be days like this, but she never said there'd be so many.
(Jack Lee, WLAK Radio, Chicago.)

● **Lender's Law.** The law of lending is to break the borrowed article.
(U/Ra.)

● **Lennie's Law of the Library.** No matter what you want, it's always on the bottom shelf.

LE CARRÉ'S ASSUMPTION

(Lennie Bemiss, Assistant Librarian, Estes Park Public Library, Estes Park, Colo.)

● **Leo's Laws.** (1) Small talk drives out meaningful talk. (2) If a song sounds like a commercial, it will become a hit. (3) The less the product the bigger the ad.
(Doug "Leo" Hanbury, Des Moines.)

● **Leonard's Constant.** There are many changes in one's life, but there is one rule that remains constant: In a men's room incoming traffic has the right of way.
(Hugh Leonard, from his play *Da.*)

● **Leveut's Cause for Rejoicing.** There is always more hell that needs raising.
(Lauren Leveut. *RA.*)

● **Levine's Declaration.** Long delays on crowded expressways are due to rubbernecking by passersby observing insignificant events. However, when I finally reach this particular point, I feel that I deserve to take time to participate in the distraction.
(Kenneth C. Levine, Doraville, Georgia.)

● **Levinson's Law No. 16.** If you check your coat at the theatre, there will be ten empty seats around you when you sit down.
(Leonard Louis Levinson, from his book *Webster's Unafraid Dictionary,* Collier Books, 1967.)

● **Lewandowski's Air Turbulence Principle.** An airline flight will remain smooth until beverage and/or meal service begins. A smooth flight will resume when beverage and/or meal service ends.
(J. A. Lewandowski, Parma, Ohio.)

● **Lewin's Deduction.** The age of our universe is a function of time.

    (Walter Lewin, Professor, MIT. Richard Stone, Stanford, Cal.)

● **Lichtenberg's Insights.** (1) If life were "just a bowl of cherries" . . . we would soon die of a deficiency disease. (2) We can never get to the Promised Land, for if we did, it would no longer be the Promised Land. (3) We say that the plow made civilization but for that matter, so did manure. (4) The zoning laws in most American neighborhoods would not *permit* the construction of a Parthenon. (5) There is no occupation as practical as love; theories are useless in bed.

    (Benjamin Lichtenberg, Verona, N.J., from his book *Insights of an Outsider,* Jaico Publishing, 1972.)

● **Liebling's News Constant.** The people who have something to say don't talk, the others insist on talking.

    (A. J. Liebling, *Holiday* magazine, February 1950.)

● **Lightfoot's Lament for Collectors of (fill in the blank).** The one time you *don't* visit a dealer, flea market, auction, or whatever, is the one time that there is an abundance of rare, fine-quality (fill in the blanks).

    (Fred Lightfoot, Greenport, N.Y.)

● **Lin's Maxim.** Happiness is a state of minimum regret.
    (Wallace E. Lin, Hartford.)

● **Lincoln's Rule of Return.** When you ask from a stranger that which is of interest only to yourself, always enclose a stamp.

    (Abraham Lincoln.)

● **Lindsay's Law.** When your draft exceeds the water's depth, you are most assuredly aground.

    (U/ME.)

● **Lindsey's Law.** The more complex a problem is, the more simple it is to resolve—in that more assumptions are available.

(Ron Lindsey, Media, Penn.)

● **Linus's Law.** There is no heavier burden than a great potential.

(From Linus, *Peanuts*. Gerald M. Fava, Lake Hiawatha, N.J.)

● **Lippmann's Law of Conformity.** When all think alike, no one thinks very much.

(Walter Lippmann. *MBC.*)

● **Lippmann's Political Rule.** [A] democratic politician had better not be right too soon. Very often the penalty is political death. It is much safer to keep in step with the parade of opinion than to try to keep up with the swifter movement of events.

(Walter Lippmann, in *The Public Philosophy*, New American Library.)

● **Lipsitt's Law.** In matters of adversity, whatever you have the most of you are going to get more of.

(Lewis P. Lipsitt, Professor of Psychology and Medical Science, Brown University. Lipsitt points out that this law is a more sophisticated version of his original discovery, which is that "One goddamned thing leads to another goddamned thing." Of his law, Lipsett says, "I have found that living by this expectation not only helps to explain for me what to others is inexplicable, but that I can proceed in my life with the clear and soothing expectation that nothing surprisingly terrible or terribly surprising is likely to happen.")

● **Liston's Dictum.** Everything eventually becomes too high priced.

    (Robert A. Liston, Shelby, Ohio.)

● **Liston's Law of Gift Wrapping.** No matter how many boxes you save, you will never have one the right size.

    (Jean Liston, Shelby, Ohio.)

● **Litt's Paradox of Deadlines.** The reason for the rush is the delay, and, conversely, the reason for the delay is the rush.

    (Lawrence Litt, Executive Editor, *The Fugue,* Miami.)

● **Livingston's Adjuration.** You can't win. Shoot for a tie.
    (E. A. Livingston, Richmond Hill, N.Y.)

● **Lloyd George's Razor.** A politician is a person with whose politics you don't agree; if you agree with him he is a statesman.

    (David Lloyd George.)

● **Lobenhofer's Law.** Any emergency sufficiently well planned for—will not happen.

    (R. W. Lobenhofer, *Modern Casting* magazine, January 1979.)

● **Lockwood's Long Shot.** The chances of getting eaten up by a lion on Main Street aren't one in a million, but once would be enough.

    (John Lockwood, Washington, D. C.)

● **Loderstedt's Rule.** Measure twice because you can only cut once.

    (Bob Loderstedt, Mendham, N.J.)

● **Loewe's Rules of Governance.** (1) If the government

hasn't taxed, licensed, or regulated it, it probably isn't worth anything. (2) The ability of the government to create money is likened to a child's desire to change the rules of a game he is losing.

(Donald C. Loewe, Chicago.)

● **Lone Eagle Law.** Before you fly make sure you're on board.

(Sign in the Lone Eagle Saloon, Minneapolis–St. Paul Airport.)

● **Long's Law of Hyphens.** In any paragraph, the number of hyphenated words is inversely proportional to the author's understanding of the relationship between the words thus hyphenated. (Examples: Indo-European, Hindu-Arabic, politico-theological, socio-economic, mathematico-physical, Judeo-Christian, and Anglo-Saxon.)

(Kevin G. Long, Quebec.)

● **Longworth's Philosophy.** Fill what's empty. Empty what's full. And scratch where it itches.

(Alice Roosevelt Longworth.)

● **Looney's Rule of Potato Chips.** You don't eat potato chips before noon.

(Douglas S. Looney, from an article on potato chips in *The American Way* magazine, December 1978.)

● **Los Angeles Dodgers Law.** Wait till last year.

(Johnny Carson, the *Tonight* show, August 2, 1979.)

● **Loughrige's Lesson.** The middle of the road is the best place to get run over.

(Alan Craig Loughrige, Springfield, Mo.)

● **Lowell's Constant.** Whatever you may be sure of, be sure of this: that you are dreadfully like other people.
(James Russell Lowell, quoted in *Catchwords of Worldly Wisdom,* [1909].)

● **Lowell's Formula.** Universities are full of knowledge; the freshmen bring a little in and the seniors take none away, and knowledge accumulates.
(Educator Abbott Lawrence Lowell.)

● **Lowell's Law of Life.** Life is a hypothesis.
(Poet Robert Lowell. *MBC.*)

● **Lubarsky's Law of Cybernetic Entomology.** There's always one more bug.
(U/DRW.)

● **Lucy's Law.** The alternative to getting old is depressing.
(U/DRW.)

● **Lynes's Law.** No author dislikes to be edited as much as he dislikes not to be published.
(Russell Lynes, from Adrian Janes, Urbana, Ill.)

● Ma Bell's Public Relations Principle. We don't care. We don't have to.

>(Bumper sticker cited by John Stephen Smith, Lincoln, Neb.)

● Ma's Rule. No matter how many pencils or pens there are in the house, none will ever be within fifteen feet of a telephone.

>*(U/Ra.)*

● McCabe's Law. Nobody HAS to do anything.
>(Charles McCabe, *San Francisco Chronicle. RS.*)

● McCarthy's Adage. The only thing that saves us from the bureaucracy is inefficiency. An efficient bureaucracy is the greatest threat to liberty.

>(Eugene McCarthy, quoted in *Time,* February 12, 1979.)

MA'S RULE

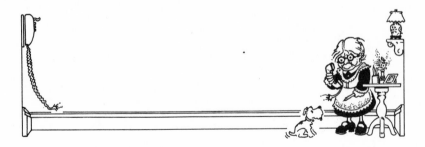

● **McGarr's First Law.** Whatever government does, it does more or less badly.

> (Judge Frank J. McGarr, U.S. District Court of Northern Illinois, from his commencement address at Loyola University Law School, June 13, 1976.)

● **McGlinchey's Law of Trust.** Never trust a world leader.
> (Herbert J. McGlinchey, former U.S. Congressman, Pennsylvania State Senator, Philadelphia ward leader from 1934 to 1976. *MBC.*)

● **McKinley's Memorial Dictum.** The worst time to ignore possible future events of high negative impact is when you are successfully building an empire and you are loved by the people.

> (In honor of William McKinley, Wayne Boucher in his article "Finding the Future," *MBA Magazine,* August/September 1978.)

● **McLaren's Motto.** Sic Transit Gloria Tuesday!
> (Jack McLaren, from *Columbo's Little Book of Canadian Proverbs, Graffiti, Limericks and Other Vital Matters* by John Robert Columbo, Hurtig Publishing, 1975.)

● **McLaughlin's Law of Walking on Railroad Ties.** They're too far for one step, but too close for two.

> (Brian McLaughlin, recorded by John Hall [c. 1953] and submitted by Hilde Weisert, Teaneck, N.J. Ms. Weisert insists that it has wide application.)

● **MacLeish's Literary Law.** If you write a novel about fruitcakes, you will hear from fruitcakes.

> (Rod MacLeish, quoted in *The Washington Post,* May 24, 1979. The discovery was occasioned by his novel, *The Man Who Wasn't There,* Random House, 1976, about a man being driven insane. He got a call from a

man in Idaho, claiming he had stolen his life story and demanding a check for $9 million.)

● **MacPherson's Working Formula.** The number of interruptions received during a work period is proportionate to the square of the number of employees occupying an office—thus, one person in an office = one interruption per hour; two in an office = four interruptions per hour; three people = nine per hour, etc.

(Ian MacPherson, Regina, Sask.)

● **Madison's Question.** If you have to travel on a *Titanic,* why not go first class?

(U/DRW.)

● **Mahr's Law of Restrained Involvement.** Don't get any on you.

*(U/*Norton Mockridge's syndicated column, February 14, 1979. *ME.)*

● **Mann's Rules.** In a corporate take-over of a well-liked cleaning product: (1) It *must* be "improved" by adding an obnoxious odor, and (2) It *must* be wrapped in a slick foil-like wrapper, to more readily slip from a wet hand.

(Mrs. Henry Mann, Holliston, Mass. *AO.*)

● **Manske's Maxim.** It doesn't matter what you do: It only matters what you say you've done and what you say you're gonna do.

(Nancy Manske, Winter Park, Fla.)

● **Mantel's First Great Law of Economics.** If two lines on a graph cross it must be important.

(U/ Ernest F. Cooke, Chairman, Marketing Department, University of Baltimore.)

● **Marguccio's Absolute.** Never buy the last item on the shelf.

(Thomas Marguccio, New York City.)

● **Marshall's Memorandum to Vice-Presidential Aspirants.** There were two brothers: One ran away to sea, and the other was elected to vice-president—and nothing was ever heard from either of them again.

(Vice-President Thomas R. Marshall.)

● **Marsolais's Law of Worst Possible Timing.** During the course of a meal, the waitress will drop by no fewer than ten times to inquire whether everything is all right; nine of those ten times your mouth will be full.

(Maurice Marsolais, Fairfax, Va.)

● **Martindale's Proverbial Logic.** [Developed from a premise stated by Dereck Williamson in *Saturday Review:* Since one picture is worth a thousand words, one word must be worth .001 of a picture.] (1) If you can lead him to water, and force him to drink, he isn't a horse. (2) The worst part of valor is indiscretion. (3) If it boils and is watched, it can't be a pot. (4) The second best policy is dishonesty. (5) If you refuse to eat the pudding, what proof have you? (6) If you are marketing a five cent cigar of high quality, you are serving admirably this country's needs.

(Canadian writer Herb Martindale, in his book, *The Caledonia Eye Opener,* Alive Press, Guelph, Ontario.)

● **Marxist Law of the Distribution of Wealth.** Shortages will be divided equally among the peasants.

(John W. Gustafson, Chicago.)

● **Mary Louise's Law.** You can't tell from where you sit when the man in the balcony will drop his program.

(Mary Louise Gabauer. *MLS.*)

● **Mary Principle, The.** If many individuals remain too long at their level of incompetence, they will destroy the organization because their presence demonstrates to others that competence is not a prerequisite for success.

> (U/J. Thomas Parry, Rockford, Ill.)

● **Masefield's R&D Rule.** The principle function of an advanced design department nowadays is to keep up with the public relations department.

> (Peter Masefield, British Aircraft managing director, quoted in Leonard Louis Levinson's *Webster's Unafraid Dictionary,* Collier Books, 1967.)

● **Maslow's Maxim.** If the only tool you have is a hammer, you treat everything like a nail.

> (Abraham Maslow, the noted psychiatrist, from Sydney J. Harris, the noted columnist. It is Harris's "favorite modern saying.")

● **Masson's Admonition.** "Be yourself!" is about the worst advice you can give some people.

> (Tom Masson, American humorist and editor.)

● **Masterson's Law** (or "The Iron Law of Wagers"). If a guy wants to bet you that he can make the Jack of Diamonds jump out of a deck of cards and spit apple cider in your ear, *don't* take that bet. Sure as shootin', you're gonna wind up with an earful of cider.

> (Sky Masterson to Nathan Detroit in *Guys and Dolls. MLS.*)

● **Matheson's Law.** Structure commands function. If you could breed an oyster the size of a horse, it wouldn't take first place in the Kentucky Derby no matter who rode it.

> (Joan Matheson, from Robert F. Tatman, Wynnewood, Penn.)

● **Matthews-Butler Principles of Plagiarism.** In the case of the first person to use an anecdote, there is originality; in the case of the second, there is plagiarism; with the third, it is lack of originality; with the fourth, it is drawing from a common stock; and in the case of the fifth, it is research.

    (Professors Brander Matthews and Nicholas Murray Butler, both of Columbia University, from *Man in the Street,* J. S. Ogilvie, publisher.)

● **Mattuck's Law.** In any given problem, difficulty is conserved, i.e., there are no true "short cuts."

    (Professor Arthur Mattuck, MIT, from Richard Stone, Stanford, Cal.)

● **Maugham's Advice.** Death is a very dull, dreary affair, and my advice to you is to have nothing whatsoever to do with it.

    (Somerset Maugham.)

● **May's Law.** The quality of the correlation is inversely proportional to the density of the control (the fewer the facts, the smoother the curves).

    (U/DRW.)

● **Mead's Law of Human Migration.** At least 50 percent of the human race doesn't want their mother-in-law within walking distance.

    (The late Margaret Mead explaining rural migration to a symposium on the phenomenon. Submitted by Paul Martin to *DRW.*)

● **Mead's Law of Problem Solving.** All major problems will be worked upon diligently until they are split into two less major problems. These will be worked on, less enthusiastically, until they are divided into four less important problems. With even less enthusiasm these four will be worked on until they are now divided into eight, again, less important problems. This subdividing of problems will continue until such time that a new major problem appears, whereupon the 32, 64, 128, or whatever now very minor problems that remain are superseded by the new "major" problem. Thus problems are never really solved, they are just broken down into minor and rather ignorable problems until such time as a new one appears.

(R. H. Mead, Ithaca, N.Y., who developed it "after some twenty-seven years in the engineering profession.")

● **Medes and Persians, Law of.** One man's Mede is another man's Persian.

(George S. Kaufman.)

Special Section 11

Medical Principles. Insights into the workings of a great profession. All but a few of these special laws were discovered/written by members of the medical community. Those with the notation *RM* were originally quoted in Dr. Robert Matz's article "Principles of Medicine," which appeared in the January 1977 issue of the *New York State Journal of Medicine*.

○ *Aronfy's Rule.* All earaches start Saturday night.
(Andrew G. Aronfy, M.D., Seabrook, Md.)
○ *Barach's Rule.* An alcoholic is a person who drinks more than his own physician.
(U/RM.)

MEAD'S LAW OF PROBLEM SOLVING

○ *FDA Law.* A drug is that substance which when injected into a rat will produce a scientific report.

   (U/RM.)

○ *Gillette's Law.* Most medical mistakes occur not from ignorance but because a physician fails to do something he or she knows should be done.

   (Robert D. Gillette, M.D., Toledo, Ohio.)

○ *Jordan's Medical Rules.* (1) Don't make two diagnoses at the same time on the same patient if you can help it; you'll probably be wrong twice. (2) They call it practicing because when you get it right, you can quit.

   (D. Wylie Jordan, M.D., Austin.)

○ *Loeb's Laws of Medicine.* (1) If what you're doing is working, keep doing it. (2) If what you're doing is not working, stop doing it. (3) If you don't know what to do, don't do anything. (4) Above all, never let a surgeon get your patient.

   (U/RM.)

○ *Lord Cohen's Aphorism.* The feasibility of an operation is not the best indication for its performance.

   (U/RM.)

○ *Marsh's Law.* Pain is always worse at night (after office hours).

   (Wallace S. Marsh, M.D., Lompoc, Cal.)

○ *Matz's General Laws.* (1) No amount of genius can overcome a preoccupation with detail. (2) Textbooks of a previous generation were as large as the textbooks of today, but contained a different body of misinformation. (3) New equipment and new procedures may improve medical care, but seldom decrease the cost. (4) Every psychoneurotic ultimately dies of organic disease.

   (From Dr. Matz's "Principles of Medicine.")

○ *Patient's Rule* (concerning his symptoms). It is not a matter of life and death—it's much more important than that.

   (U/RM.)

○ *Rogawski's Laws of Medical Science.* (1) A paper supporting any claim can be found somewhere in medical literature. (2) For any published paper, there is a paper giving opposite conclusions.

> (Michael A. Rogawski, Department of Pharmacology, Yale University.)

○ *Shem's Laws of the House of God* (a selection). (1) At a cardiac arrest, the first procedure is to take your own pulse. (2) The patient is the one with the disease. (3) If you don't take a temperature, you can't find a fever.

> (From the novel *The House of God,* by Samuel Shem, M.D., Richard Marek, 1978. Shem is the pseudonym for a young physician.)

○ *White's Rule.* The effectiveness of a therapy for a disease is inversely proportional to the number of therapies available to treat the disease.

> (Robert I. White, Jr., M.D., The Johns Hopkins University School of Medicine. Dr. White amplifies, "Instead of therapy, one might substitute drugs, etc. Good examples of this would be the wide variety of non-narcotic pain medicines or common cold remedies. The reverse, of course, is that if a patient has appendicitis, there is only one therapy, namely, appendectomy, which is extremely effective.")

● **Meller's Six Sociological Laws.** (1) Anyone who can be exploited will be. (2) If you understand the direction of the flow of money, you can predict human conduct. From this it follows that if you can control the direction of the flow of money, you can control human conduct. Man is like a sailboat and the flow of money is the wind. (3) Anything based on greed and avarice is on a firm foundation and will prevail. (4) Everyone feels that he is underpaid and overcharged. (5) For every human act there are two reasons—the stated one and the real one. These two have a correlation coefficient that varies from one to zero. (6) We have more to fear from the bungling of the incompetent than from the machinations of the wicked.

> (R. L. Meller, M.D., Minneapolis. From J. Thomas Parry, who states: "Dr. Meller is a psychiatrist and after many, many years of practice developed these laws. Dr. Meller states with conviction that these are the only laws necessary to understand human behavior.")

Memorandum.

From: Author
To: Reader
Subject: Meaning in Memos

1. In large organizations, memos are rewritten at each major hierarchical level.
2. Each rewrite changes the meaning of the memo . . .
3. . . . until it is either (a) meaningless, (b) silly, or (c) both of the above.
4. Case in point: In 1977 President Carter penned a memo to the effect that more federal money should be spent at the retail level with minority businesses. A year later, when the memo got to a small government group in Baltimore, the people in the office were told (a) they should fill out a report every time they bought gasoline with government money and note whether or not it was from a minority-owned station, and (b) they could not ask if a member of a minority owned the station for fear of offending.

● **Mencken's Rule of Unanimity.** When everyone begins to believe anything it ceases to be true; for example, the notion that the homeliest girl in the party is the safest.
(H. L. Mencken.)

● **Mendoza's Laws of Purchasing.** (1) When shopping, never look for something specific, you won't find it. (2) Always shop for nothing, you'll always come back with something. (3) After a heavy day's shopping, the perfect purchase is in either the first or the last place you've looked.
(Liz Mendoza, Fargo, N.D.)

● **Merrow's Law.** Optimism tends to expand to fill the scope available for its exercise.
(Edward Merrow, RAND Corp. economist, who uses his law to describe synthetic fuel enthusiasts. *RS.*)

● **Metropolitan Edison's Variation on Murphy's Law.** Anything that man makes will not operate perfectly.
(Walter M. Creitz, President of Metropolitan Edison, the company that operates the Three Mile Island nuclear plant. Quoted in *The New York Times,* March 30, 1979.)

● **Metzger's Maxim.** You're only as old as you feel—the next day.
(Daniel J. Metzger, Belleville, Ill.)

● **Miazga's Discovery.** Death is nature's way of telling you the FDA was right.
(Robert Miazga, Danbury, Conn.)

● **Midas's Law.** Possession diminishes perception of value, immediately.
(John Updike, *The New Yorker,* November 3, 1975.)

● **Mikadet's Cardinal Rule for Parents of Adult Children.** An eighteen-year-old can: (a) vote, (b) rebuild an automobile engine, (c) swallow a guitar pick.
(T. K. Mikadet, Lompoc, Cal.)

● **Miles's Political Prayer.** Yea, even though I graze in pastures with Jackasses, I pray that I will not bray like one.
(William Miles, Anna Marie, Fla.)

● **Miller's Corollary.** Objects are lost because people look where they are not instead of where they are.
(Henry L. Miller, London.)

● **Miller's Distinction.** There is a thin line of distinction between the avant-garde and *The Gong Show*.
(U/Ra.)

● **Miller's Law.** All costs walk on two legs.
(Arjay Miller. From Hal Hoverland, Dean, California State College, San Bernardino.)

● **Mills's Law.** The ease by which a man can be convinced, by artful manipulation of language, of something contrary to common sense, is directly proportional to his advance in philosophy.
(J. S. Mills, *A System of Logic, Book 3*. From Kevin G. Long, Quebec.)

● **Mills's Law.** There is no task so great that it cannot be done in one night.
(This law—created by Patty Mills, Mount Holyoke College, 1964, and submitted by Hilde Weisert—points out that it seems to work better in college than in "life after college.")

● **Mirsky's Law of Auditioning.** If they say "Thank you," you've got a shot. . . . If they say "Thank you very much," forget it.

(Steven D. Mirsky, Ithaca, N.Y.)

Special Section 12

Miseries of 1806. In the early days of the 19th century, a cluster of half a dozen or so books appeared in England with the key word "miseries" in their titles. Each small volume was written pseudonymously and contained a series of "groans" attesting to the conspiracy of events, objects, and other humans that kept the authors in, as one put it, "a frenzy of vexation."

These books are desperately hard to find today, but through the Library of Congress two classics of the genre—both published in 1806—have been found and will shortly be quoted from. The importance of rediscovering these miseries is simply that the books give us clear proof that the so-called curses of modernism predate the Modern Era and the knowledge of the inherent perversity of things has been a constant for longer than we commonly realize. Enough preamble. Let us move on to some of the specific miseries cited in two early Murphylogical classics, *The Miseries of Human Life or the Groans of Samuel Sensitive and Timothy Testy* by Samuel Sensitive and Timothy Testy (Wm. Miller, London, 1806) and *More Miseries!! Addressed to the Morbid, the Melancholy and the Irritable* by Sir Fretful Murmur (H. D. Symonds, London, 1806).*

---

*Some scholarly scratching leads to the conclusion that Sensitive and Testy were one man, James Beresford of Merton College, Oxford, and that Murmur was a writer named Robert Heron.

MISERIES OF 1806

■All your acquaintance telling you, that a portrait which you are aware is *rather flattering,* is not at all like you.

■Being requested by a foreigner who understands very little of the English language, to hear him read Milton.

■Calling on a sultry day upon a friend who has the mania for planting upon him; who marches and countermarches you three or four miles to see his plantations, after which he irresistibly presses you to ascend a *considerable eminence of ground,* about half a mile off, to see a couple of pines which he planted on the day his first child was born.

■Attempting, at a strange house, to take down a book from a high, crowded shelf, bringing the library upon your nose.

■As an author—those moments during which you are relieved from the fatigues of composition by finding that your memory, your intellects, your imagination, your spirits, and even your love of the subject, have all, as if with one consent, left you in the lurch.

■Writing with ink of about the consistency of pitch, which leaves alternatively a blot and a blank.

■Writing upon a thin sheet of paper, very small crumbs of bread under it.

■Looking for a good pen (which is your personal destiny never to find, except when you are indifferent about it), and having a free choice among the following varieties:

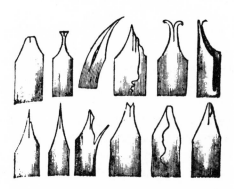

■ Having a pimple on your chin, covering it with sticking plaster, and just as you enter the drawing room, discovering that it curls on all sides.

■ Being bored by a man whom you don't like, to dine with him, and being nailed by his begging you to fix your own day.

■ Living in chambers under a man who takes private lessons in dancing.

■ Sitting at dinner next to a man of consequence with whom you wish to ingratiate yourself, being told that he has superstitious horror of the salt being spilt, and from excess of caution sending the contents of the salt cellar into his plate.

■ Whilst you are making a sketch, having a number of impertinent persons staring behind you, until the crowd increases to that degree that you are obliged to abandon your subject.

■ Asking a lady to permit you to look at a beautiful string of very small pearls, breaking it in two, scattering them over the floor, and crushing several under your feet in endeavouring to collect them.

■ Toasting a bit of bread at the end of a short dessert fork, before a good brisk fire, and burning the ends of your fingers without being able to toast it to your liking.

■ Having succeeded in fixing yourself in a most seducing, and graceful attitude, letting your cocked hat fall.

■ Knocking at a door, and by a horrible and unaccountable lapse of memory, forgetting the name of the master or mistress of the house.

■ Upon paying the first visit after the funeral of a relation, a distant cousin for instance, to the immediate friends of the deceased, finding them all in tears from some unaccountable counteraction of nature, and not being able to look grave upon the occasion.

■ Upon returning from a Tour to the Continent, being asked by everyone you meet for *your private opinion of things in general.*

■ Trying to pass a man who waddles.

■ Being requested to say something to entertain the party.

■Sitting for your portrait to a subordinate painter who renders the likeness with such exasperating exactness, that every pimple, blotch and blemish in the face are faithfully represented.

■Striking your foot against another step after you had concluded that you had reached the top of the stairs.

■Being seized with a violent bowel complaint, whilst you are riding on horseback with two young ladies, to one of whom you are paying your addresses, being obliged to alight in great confusion, telling your fair companions, that there is an exquisite bit of scenery round a hedge, and which you should like very much to sketch, assuring them that you will return in five minutes, and remembering afterwards that it was well known that you never drew in your life.

(These are but a few of hundreds of miseries catalogued by these pioneers. It boggles the mind to consider what they could have come up with if they had been alive for the coming of the telephone, IRS Form 1040, computer, television, automobile, superhighway, and other elements of human progress.)

● **MIST Law** (Man in the Street). The number of people watching you is directly proportional to the stupidity of your action.

(U/DRW.)

● **Mitchell's Rustic Rule.** Changing barnyards will not transform a turkey into a golden goose.

(Kevin Mitchell, Eden Prairie, Minn.)

● **Miz Beaver's Summation of Walt Kelly's Philosophy.** He allus said, don't take life too serious . . . it ain't nohow permanent.

(Miz Beaver, in the *Pogo* comic strip, the Christmas following Walt Kelly's death.)

● **Mockridge's Major Maxim.** If an idea is successful, the first person to claim credit for it will be the person who contended all along that it wouldn't work!
(Syndicated columnist Norton Mockridge.)

● **Modell's Laws.** (1) Nothing is so serious that it can't be teased until it is ragged at the edges. (2) Nothing is so simple that it cannot be made too complex to work.
(U/GT.)

● **Momma's Rule.** If you can't stand to eat, get out of my kitchen.
(From the comic strip *Momma* by Mell Lazarus.)

● **Money Maxim.** Money isn't everything. (It isn't plentiful, for instance.)
(Bill Woods, *DRW*'s father.)

● **Montgomery's Explanation of the Facts of Life.** All normal young people want to do this thing. It is natural, like fighting.
(Attributed to Lord Montgomery.)

● **Montore's Maxims.** (1) A true environmentalist will use both sides of a piece of paper in presenting a position paper. (2) Every journey, great and small, begins with unrealistic expectations. (3) Love expands to fill the available hearts. (4) Man's superiority to the rest of the animal kingdom is due primarily to his imagination. He imagines he is superior. (5) No balls, no blue chips.
(R. J. Montore, Henderson, Ky.)

● **Moore's Constant.** Everybody sets out to do something, and everybody does something, but no one does what he sets out to do.

(Irish novelist George Moore.)

● **Moore's Law.** The degree to which a topic is understood is inversely proportional to the amount of literature available on it. *Corollary:* That which seems vague is frequently meaningless.

(Terry C. Moore, Indianapolis, Indiana. Moore finds widespread application of this law and corollary in fields as diverse as child rearing, business management, macroeconomic theory, and Transactional Analysis.)

● **Morford's Rule.** Nothing fails like success.

(Ida B. Morford, Glassboro State College, Glassboro, N.J. Submitted by Rose Primack, one of Dr. Morford's colleagues, who says it came out of a postmortem on a "highly successful environmental education program that was almost universally applauded" when it was discontinued.)

● **Moriarity's Secret for Financial Success.** BLASH.

(Named for a highly successful investment broker named Morton P. Moriarity, who was once one of the biggest failures on Wall Street. When destitute and reduced to sleeping on park benches he had a dream in which a bearded holy man handed him a piece of paper with the word BLASH on it. Moriarity ran all around New York in search of a bearded holy man who could tell him what BLASH meant; finally, after a year-long search, he found his man, who told him it stood for "Buy Low and Sell High." This, from Carl Winston's book *How to Run a Million into a Shoestring and Other Shortcuts to Success,* G. P. Putnam's Sons, 1960.)

● **Morley's Advice to Travelers.** Avoid plays acted in a foreign language, and buildings entirely rebuilt since the war.

Beware of government-sponsored stores and light operas. Limit yourself to one cathedral, one picture gallery, and one giant Buddha a week.

(Actor Robert Morley, from *A Musing Morley,* edited by Sheridan Morley.)

● **Morris's Law.** When writing in ink, you never make a mistake until you are at least three-fourths of the way through.

(John C. Morris, Jr., Old Greenwich, Conn. Morris, believed to be the youngest of all Murphy Center Fellows, is a fifth-grade student in the Greenwich public schools. The law was forwarded by Annie C. Harvey, one of his teachers.)

● **Morris's Laws of Animal Appeal.** (1) The popularity of an animal is directly correlated with the number of anthropomorphic features it possesses. (2) The age of a child is inversely correlated with the size of the animals it prefers.

(Desmond Morris from *The Naked Ape,* McGraw-Hill, 1967.)

● **Morris's Tips for Beginning Writers (a selection).** (1) Although most magazines maintain that they pay so much a word, virtually none of them will buy words submitted individually. Keep this in mind, and your mailing costs will nose-dive. (2) To sell inspirational pieces and "cute" poems, you *must* have a three-part name, preferably Elyse McBride Sensenbrenner. (3) The placing of Happy Face stickers on or about your manuscript does not measurably enhance its appeal.

(Edward Morris, in his article "Keeping the Crayons Sharp," *Writer's Digest,* December 1977.)

● **Morrison's Last Theorem.** If you hang in there long enough and grit your teeth hard enough, your orthodontist bill will go up.

(Stan Morrison, retired basketball coach, University of the Pacific, quoted in *Sports Illustrated.* From Michael L. Lazare, Armonk, N.Y.)

● **Morrison's Second-Sheet Law.** When you are doing two copies of anything, the carbon always turns out better than the original.
(Vivian M. Morrison, Shreveport, Louisiana.)

● **Moutsatson's Law.** If you don't do anything—you can't do anything wrong.
(Pete Moutsatson, Chairman, Business Studies Department, Montcalm Community College, Sidney, Mich.)

● **Moynihan's Maxim.** Whenever any branch of the government acquires a new technique which enhances its power in relation to the other branches, that technique will soon be adopted by those other branches as well.
(Senator Daniel P. Moynihan. *AO.*)

● **Muir's Golden Rule of Menus.** If you can't pronounce it, you can't afford it.
(Frank Muir, in *The English Digest.*)

● **Muir's Law.** If it's right and you've checked that it's right, you can be sure someone will come along and correct you.
(Georgette Muir, New York City.)

● **Muldoon-Becker Rules.** (1) Software, when left unattended, rots! (2) Thank God it's Friday—only two more working days this week.
(Ed Muldoon and Nick Becker, Des Plaines, Ill.)

Special Section 13

Murphylogical Research, Recent Findings. (An interview with the Director of the Murphy Center.)

[Q] The Center's interest in the prophet Murphy and the many laws attributed to him and named in his honor is, of course, keen. Yet there still seems to be some question as to who Murphy actually was or is. Do you have any new discoveries to report?

[A] Yes. As you may recall from the Center's last report *(The Official Rules,* Delacorte, 1978) it was tentatively concluded that the great Murphy was a military man, Capt. Ed Murphy, who first announced the basic law of "If anything can go wrong it will" in 1949. Other Murphylogical scholars came to the same conclusion. But now new evidence has come to the Center's attention posing some intriguing new possibilities.

[Q] The suspense is too much. What are they?

[A] The first comes from Theodore C. Achilles. I shall quote directly from his letter to the Center:

Many people believe that the real author was the late Ambassador Robert Murphy. During his career of more than forty years in the Foreign Service during which he served, in addition to many other trouble spots, in Hitler's Germany, Laval's France, immediate postwar Germany, he accumulated monumental evidence of its validity. I suspect he formulated it definitively at the end of the 1930s. In the late 1920s as a young Vice Consul in Munich, he and his friend Msgr. Pacelli, Apostolic Delegate to Bavaria, spent an evening in a *bierstube* listening to the ranting of a young man named Adolf Hitler. After the speech and a few steins they agreed to report to their respective authorities that the young man was merely a blowhard who was unlikely to have any significant effect on events in Germany or anywhere else. Some years later, after Pacelli had become Pope Pius XII, Bob gently reminded him of their consensus. "Ah yes," replied His Holiness, "that was before I became infallible."

Another body of evidence has reached the Center to the effect that the basic law and Murphy's name were well known during the early days of World War II. Charlie Boone, of the incomparable Boone-Ericson radio show in Minneapolis, testifies to this point: "The inspiration may go back to the training camps of World War II or earlier. At the Infantry Training School at Fort Benning, Georgia, in 1942, almost every demonstration group included a Private Murphy. In the serious business of training officers, Private Murphy provided comic relief, for he never failed to take the wrong action, make the wrong decision. His negative action often reinforced the instructor's teacher better than any school solutions or field manuals could."

Still another batch of suggestions come from those who insist that, regardless of who Murphy was, the basic principle dates back centuries to a number of sources including Julius Caesar, who once said, *"Quod malum posset futurum,"* which turns out to be Murphy's Law roughly translated. Others suggest that Murphy lies within our collective ages-old consciousness and that variations and corollaries of Murphy's Law can be found in the proverbs of many cultures: "The spot always falls on the best cloth" (Spanish), "The hidden stone finds the plow" (Estonian), and "One always knocks oneself on the sore place" (English).

Q. Fascinating. Are there more?

A. Just one. But the one I think is the best explanation to date. James V. Stewart of St. Petersburg, Florida, is the person who uncovered it. Let me quote from his letter:

> Murphy's Law was first formulated by Samuel Beckett in his novel named, of course, *Murphy,* which was first published in 1938.
>
> As I'm sure you are aware, there is no way I would be

able to know if Beckett's book is, in fact, the origin of Murphy's Law; nevertheless, Beckett's reference to "If anything can go wrong, it will" is earlier than any other that you cite as possible origins, so I thought you might appreciate being placed on notice.

For this wonderful bit of scholarship, the Center is bestowing on Mr. Stewart the coveted title of Fellow.

[Q.] Now that we've settled that issue . . .

[A.] Hold on. No research center worth its salt ever truly settles an issue, because if it did, it would soon run out of issues and put itself out of business. As befits a modern American think tank, the only true conclusion we have reached is that the need for further research is indicated.

[Q.] Pardon me. On to other matters. Has the Center discovered any new variations and corollaries to Murphy's Law?

[A.] Scores of them—some universal and some that have been adapted to the realities of a certain profession or pursuit. For instance, the Center has received so many computer-related variations on Murphy's Law that it has decided against buying one. Here are some of our new acquisitions:

○ *Mrs. Murphy's Law.* Anything that can go wrong will go wrong WHILE HE IS OUT OF TOWN.
> (Mrs. Murphy, Valrico, Fla., quoted in Ann Landers's column of May 9, 1978.)

○ *Murphy's Constant.* All constants are variables.
> *(U/Ra.)*

○ *Murphy's Hope.* Today's "hopefully" is tomorrow's "It had been hoped."
> (Sal Rosa, New York City)

○ *Murphy's Law of Product Geography.* The extent of problems with any new product varies directly as the distance between buyer and seller.
> *(ME.)*

o *NBC's Addendum to Murphy's Law.* You never run out of things that can go wrong.

> (Associated Press Television writer Peter J. Boyer, in his
> column for August 3, 1979, on NBC's problems.)

One of the most comprehensive codifications we have ever seen has to do with Murphy and marketing, which appeared in *Mainly Marketing: The Schoonmaker Report to the Electronics Industry* published by Schoonmaker Associates of Coram, N.Y., and which contains approximately sixty-five Murphylogical dictums. A small sampling:

o *Advertising*

. . . The longer management delays in approving a radically new campaign, the greater the odds that a competitor will preempt the basic concept.

. . . The larger the group and the higher the rank of agency members pitching a prospect, the lower the rank and the smaller the team serving the account after the contract has been signed.

o *Market Planning*

. . . In planning a related product family, the least amount of attention will be paid to the model that will prove most popular. It will prove to be impossible to meet the demand by modifying other members of the family.

. . . The more smoothly a complicated plan runs at the start, the deeper and more intricate the problems will be once the point of no return has been passed.

o *Market Research*

. . . The most academically sound survey design will yield findings in terms that are least usable (such as sales in dollars when units are needed).

o *Sales*

. . . Psychological testing that is 80 percent accurate will assign members of the 20 percent group to the most sensitive territories and accounts.

. . . The more cordial the buyer's secretary, the greater the odds that competition already has the order.

Q. Is there any evidence to show that the force of Murphy's Law is growing?

A. You jest. How else can one find any suitable explanation for the recent past—Watergate, the Department of Energy, the swine flu vaccine, OPEC, the "vast promise" of nuclear energy, metric conversion, tax reform, the WIN program, the gas line, the Ayatollah, and so much more. On a more workaday level it is the only way that one can explain the fact that if you left here and went to a supermarket, you would immediately gravitate to a shopping cart with either a square wheel or a wheel that is pointed in a direction that is precisely 90 degrees from the other three.

One of the things that the Center is working on right now is a collection of incidents that perfectly illustrate the law in action. Frank S. Preston of the University of North Carolina has discovered an example that fits this category of "perfect." As he reports, "One of the best cases I know of involves a World War II German airplane that was hung from the ceiling of the Smithsonian Institution for exhibit. Although this airplane survived World War II unscratched, it has crashed twice inside the Smithsonian. . . ."

Now, one of my pet instances is contained in this little clipping I carry around in my wallet. Listen to this, "Brian Chellender, twenty-nine, a bricklayer, was bending down to pick up a pin for good luck, whereupon he was knocked unconscious by a falling brick . . ."

Q. Hold on a second. This strikes me as somewhat depressing —downright depressing, actually—all of this dwelling on things that backfire.

A. Not so. You have missed the point of the Law and the Center. The very fact that there is a Center that sorts, studies, and helps formalize all of this is as uplifting as—and I hate to admit this—a Jaycee Awards dinner or—more painful to admit—those silly smile faces that some people stick on their letters. You see that laying off all of these gaffs, flubs, and mis-cues on universal law is ultimately reassuring and comforting.

In all of our lives, there is the raw material to prove Murphy's Law or one of its corollaries, an amazing example of shared humanity. Rather than deny all of this, the Center celebrates the universal and unlimited imperfectibility of people, organizations, and objects.

Q. Is the Center doing research on this?

A. Of course, one of the things we're working on right now is the "Theory of the Perverse Wind." Specifically, we have evidence that we think will eventually prove there is a particular wind that dies the minute you try to launch a kite, starts up when you drop a $20 bill, and gives off a tiny puff when you are taping something, thereby forcing the tape to stick to itself.

Q. Very interesting. Anything else?

A. Much more. Just to give you an idea of some of the things under investigation here, I'll quickly list some of the specific elements of the Center's research agenda:

Zipper behavior.

Telehydrotropism (or, in lay language, the ability of wrong numbers to ring when one is taking a bath).

The reproductive ability of wire coat hangers.

The aerodynamics and camouflage of the contact lens.

Child-proof aspirin bottles that have the ability to incense adults with hangovers and refuse to open for them.

Calculators that only go out during final exams and the day before taxes are due.

Pocket genetics—trying to unlock the secret that will explain why your grandfather's fountain pen leaked in his pocket, why your father's ballpoint pen leaked in his pocket, and why your marker pen leaks in your pocket.

Key telekinesis—the supernatural process by which everyone gets a mystery key on their key ring that doesn't fit anything.

The origin of that wonderful, universal hospital custom whereby patients are wakened from a sound sleep to take a sleeping pill.

Finally, I should mention that we have one large-scale research project which has just started. Called "Project Hercules," it is a

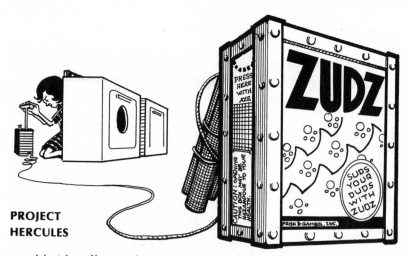

**PROJECT
HERCULES**

worldwide effort enlisting all of the Center's Fellows. We are trying to see if anyone, anywhere, has actually performed certain fabled superhuman feats. For instance, we're combing the globe to find someone who has actually opened a detergent box by following the instructions, "Press flap gently, lift and pull back." Tests at our secret lab have required a minimum of one chisel, a heavy rock, and an electric saber saw to manage this. Another top priority is finding someone who has completed one of those "easy weekend" projects in the home-oriented magazines in less than a month of Sundays.

● **Murray's Laws.** (1) Cars with the lucky pieces hanging off the rearview mirror will always seem to star in bad accidents. (2) You can fool all of the people all of the time—if you own the network. (3) If everything else fails, throw it away.

(Jim Murray of the *Los Angeles Times,* from his column of November 23, 1978.)

● **Mykia's Law.**

> Has anyone, since the birth of the nation,
> On dropping the bathroom soap,
> Retrieved it not in need of depilation?

(Mykia Taylor, Glenside, Penn.)

N

● **Napier's Discovery.** In the past 200 years, America has manufactured close to 100 billion pencils—and we still can't keep one by the phone.

(Arch Napier, from *The Wall Street Journal.*)

● **NASA Skylab Rule.** Don't do it if you can't keep it up.

(Johnny Carson, the *Tonight* show, August 2, 1979.)

● **Nathan-Dommel Law of Federal Grants.** Given the chance, governments will spread benefits so as to provide something for everybody.

(Richard Nathan and Paul Dommel, "Understanding the Urban Predicament," *The Brookings Bulletin,* 14:1–2, 1977.)

● **Nelson's Law.** Negative thinking never got nobody nothing.

(Bert Nelson, Los Altos, Cal.)

● **Nelson's Theory of the Dead End.** Everybody at a party will sift into the room that has only one door, no matter how small or cramped.

(Designer George Nelson, quoted in *The Washington Post,* July 2, 1978. *JCG.*)

● **Nevitsky's Observation.** If a tedious job requires a certain rhythm so that it can be performed quickly and efficiently, that rhythm will be broken immediately upon psychological realization of the rhythm.

(William C. Callis, Falls Church, Va.)

● **Newell's Truisms.** (1) Whenever possible analyze planned performance—actuals are too elusive. (2) A cumulative impact never equals the sum of its increments.

(Roger Newell, Webster, N.Y.)

● **Newman's Law.** Hypocrisy is the Vaseline of social intercourse.

(U/DRW.)

● **Nock's Grim Truth.** In proportion as you give the State power to do things for you, you give it power to do things to you; and the State invariably makes as little as it can of the one power, and as much as it can of the other.

(Albert Jay Nock from his *Memoirs of a Superfluous Man,* Regnery, 1964. *JMcC.* Nock is also the author of the next item.)

● **Nock's Sad Reminder.** The hope for any significant improvement of society must be postponed, if not forever, at any rate to a future so far distant that consideration of it at the present time would be sheer idleness.

● **Nolan's Law.** If you outsmart your lawyer, you've got the wrong lawyer.

(Attorney John T. Nolan, Iowa City, Iowa.)

● **Nonreciprocal Law of Expectation and Results.** Positive expectations yield negative results. Negative expectations yield negative results.

(*U*/Richard B. Bernstein.)

● **Norris's Advice.** Always err on the side of truth.

(Ken S. Norris, Professor of Natural History, Santa Cruz, Cal.)

● **North's Law of Investment Advisors.**
There are some extremely sharp investment advisors
who can get you in at the bottom of the market.
There are some extremely sharp ones who can get
you out at the top.
They are never the same people.
Corollary: You will act on the advice of the wrong one
at least 50 percent of the time.
(Gary North, Executive Director, American Bureau of Economic Research, Durham, N.C.)

● **Norvell's Reminder.** If you would be remembered, do
one thing superbly well.
(Saunders Norvell. *ME.*)

● **Notes from a Life in Progress (A Selection).** ■ Science
has proven that within the breast of every organism of field
mouse rank or higher there beats the desire someday to shout
"Stop the presses!"■ Money in a wallet tends to be spent.■ The
best and the worst make history. The mediocre breed.■ Saints
always muck up the demographics.
(Ryan Anthony, Tucson.)

● **Novinson's Revolutionary Discovery.** When comes the
Revolution, things will be different—not better, just different.
(Ronald M. Novinson, Alexandria, Va.)

● **Novotney's Law of Correctives.** Whenever a practice
or procedure is finally seen to be irrational and intolerable, the
practice or procedure instituted to correct the situation will be
equally irrational. *Corollary:* Every practice or procedure is actually irrational; it is only a matter of time until it is seen to be so.
(Andrew J. Novotney, S.J., Rockhurst College, Kansas
City, Mo.)

● **Nursing Mother Principle.** Do not nurse a kid who wears braces.

(Johnny Carson, the *Tonight* show, August 2, 1979.)

● **Nye's Maxim.** Kind words will never die—neither will they buy groceries.

("Bill" Nye, nineteenth-century American humorist.)

● **Obis's Law.** Someone else probably has the same idea —so (a) get started, (b) plan to do it better.
(Paul Obis, Jr., Milford, Conn.)

● **O'Brien's Law of Take-out Food.** No matter what or how much you order, it always takes twenty minutes.
(Edward L. O'Brien, Washington, D.C.)

● **Obvious Law.** Actually, it only *seems* as though you mustn't be deceived by appearances.
(Donald R. Woods, Stanford, Cal.)

● **O'Connor's Dicta.** (1). In any classroom, the question is always more important than the answer. *Corollary:* The necessity of providing an answer varies inversely with the amount of time the question can be evaded. (2). In any piece of electronic equipment, it is foolhardy to assume that jiggling "X" will not diddle "Y", however unlikely.
(Vincent D. O'Connor, Winona, Minn.)

● **Oddo's Axiom.** *Never* say you don't know—nod wisely, leave calmly, then run like hell to find an expert.
(S.M. Oddo, San Diego, Cal.)

Special Section 14

Official Diagrams. Important concepts rendered graphically.

1. One Round Tuit.

CUT OUT AND KEEP! At long last we have a sufficient quantity of these for all personnel to have their own. Guard it with your life. Never lose it, and don't let anyone take it away from you.

These tuits have been hard to come by, especially the round version. We are glad to have them because the demand has been great, and now many of our problems concerning reports and really getting things accomplished in this organization will be solved.

We look for productivity to double in every section now that each of you has his own round tuit. As so many of you have said, "I will get started on this just as soon as I get a round tuit." Others have complained, "I know the job should be done, but I just haven't been able to get a round tuit."

2. Hanging a Swing—Educational Version.

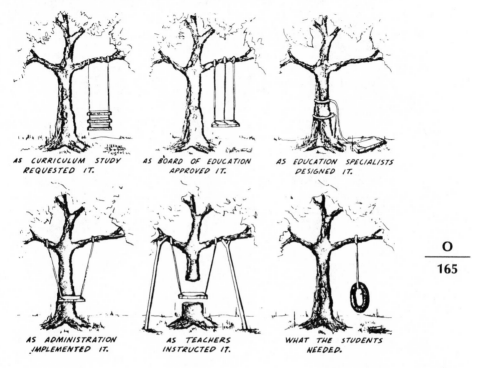

AS CURRICULUM STUDY REQUESTED IT.

AS BOARD OF EDUCATION APPROVED IT.

AS EDUCATION SPECIALISTS DESIGNED IT.

AS ADMINISTRATION IMPLEMENTED IT.

AS TEACHERS INSTRUCTED IT.

WHAT THE STUDENTS NEEDED.

(There are many variations on the swings diagram. In the business version, for instance, the swings are labeled [*left to right*]: "As marketing requested it," "As sales ordered it," "As engineering designed it," "As production manufactured it," "As plant installed it," and "What the customer wanted.")

3. Rush Job Calendar.
1. Every job is in a rush. Everyone wants his job yesterday. With this calendar, a customer can order his work on the *seventh* and have it delivered on the *third*.

NEG	FRI	FRI	THU	WED	TUE	MON
8	7	6	5	4	3	2
16	15	14	13	12	11	9
23	22	21	20	19	18	17
31	30	29	28	27	26	24
38	37	36	35	34	33	32

2. All customers want their jobs on *Friday* so there are *two Fridays* in every week.

3. There are seven days at the end of the month for those end-of-the-month jobs.

4. There will be no first-of-the-month bills to be paid, as there isn't any "first." The "tenth" and "twenty-fifth" have also been omitted in case you have been asked to pay them one of those days.

5. There are no bothersome nonproductive Saturdays and Sundays. No time-and-a-half or double-time to pay.

6. There's a new day each week called negotiation day.

4. Organization Chart: Heaven.

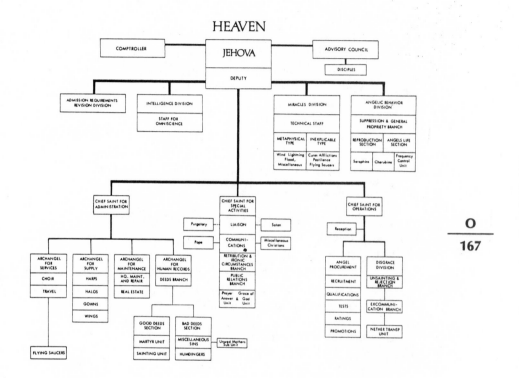

● **Official Explanations, Law of.** When the word "Official" is used in conjunction with an explanation, it can only follow that the explanation is unwittingly wrong, a half-truth, or an outright lie.

(This law is rediscovered with each major crisis, but seldom has it returned with such ferocity as it did during the Three Mile Island nuclear incident. Within forty-eight-hours of the initial problem there were seven different official explanations.)

● **Ogden's Law.** The sooner you fall behind, the more time you have to catch up.

(Sam Ogden, Amherst, Mass. From the Letters section, *Time,* March 19, 1979.)

● **Olbers's Paradox.** The contradictory fact that the sky is dark at night, although by all calculations involving star radiance it should be as bright as the surface of the sun.

(German astronomer Wilhelm Olbers [1758–1840]. This is a useful bit of information to employ when calculated reality and reality don't jibe.)

● **Old Boy's Law.** You don't learn anything the second time you're kicked by a mule.

(U / Ra.)

● **Old's Conclusion.** The peaking of the output of a committee versus the number of committee members [is] seven-tenths of a person. Obviously one must conclude that either further research is required or that people are no damned good.

(Bruce S. Old, in his 1946 *Scientific Monthly* article "On the Mathematics of Committees, Boards and Panels.")

● **Old Doc Moos's Law.** When it is necessary to choose between ignorance and stupidity, choose ignorance. It is curable.

(Phil Moos, M.D., St. Cloud, Minn.)

LAW OF OFFICIAL EXPLANATIONS

● **Old Fraternity Meeting Rule.** The time spent at a fraternity meeting discussing any matter is inversely proportional to the significance of the matter discussed. For example, the theme for the next house party will be discussed for hours, whereas whether the fraternity should abandon its charter will occupy only a few minutes of discussion.

(A. S. Boccuti, Baltimore.)

● **Olly's Observation.** The tap water is always coldest after you have finished your drink.

(W. A. "Olly" Herold, Islington, Ont.)

● **Olmstead's Law.** After all is said and done, a hell of a lot more is said than done.

(Clark Olmstead, Hanau, West Germany.)

● **Olsen's Necktie Law.** The only way to prevent getting food on your necktie is to put it in the refrigerator.

(U/Ra.)

● **Omar's Maxim.** The smaller the country, the greater the passport formalities.

(Margaret K. Omar, U.S. Embassy, Tunis.)

● **O'Neill's Observation.** Nobody is too old to learn—but a lot of people keep putting it off.

(William O'Neill, Diamond Bar, Cal.)

● **Orben's Ornithological Statistic.** There are 40 million pigeons in the United States—30 million are birds, and the rest are people who pay $40 for designer blue jeans.

(Bob Orben, Arlington, Va.)

● **Organizational Parable.**
Once upon a time there was a handsome young lion. He

was captured in the African jungle and brought to America, where he was put on display in a zoo. This made the lion very unhappy because he preferred the freedom of his wild native land and the companionship of other jungle beasts. But after a time he became resigned to his fate and made up his mind that if he had to live behind bars he would be the best zoo lion around.

In an adjoining cage there was another lion, an old and lazy one with a negative responsibility and no signs of ambition or capability of any kind. He lay all day in the sun, aroused no interest from visitors. In sharp contrast, the young lion paced for hours back and forth in his cage. He acted the true King of Beasts, rolling his maned head, snarling, and baring his teeth. The crowds loved him. They paid no attention to the indolent old lion asleep in the next cage.

The young lion appreciated the attention he was getting, but he was annoyed by his failure to win adequate reward. Each afternoon the zoo keeper came through the cages to feed the animals. The lazy old lion, who made no effort to please the spectators, was given a big bowl of red horsemeat. The young lion, now a star attraction, was given a bowl of chopped-up oranges, bananas, and nuts. This made him very unhappy.

"Perhaps," he mused, "I am not trying hard enough. I will improve the act." So he strutted longer and more spectacularly. To the snarls and gnashing of teeth he added frequent roars that shook the bars of his cage. The crowds got bigger. Thousands of citizens came to see his performance, and he was pictured on page one in the local newspaper.

But the diet did not change. Still the lazy lion got the red meat, and the young lion stayed on a vegetarian diet. Finally he could endure it no longer. He stopped the keeper with a challenge.

"I am getting sick and tired of this," he complained. "Each day you give that no-good lazy type next door a big bowl of meat, and you feed me oranges, bananas, and nuts. It is grossly unfair. Why do you think all these people come to the zoo? They come to see me. I'm the star attraction, the lion that's doing all the work, and the one that gets the results. Why am I not entitled to meat for dinner?"

The keeper did not hesitate with his reply.

"Young man," he said, "you don't know how lucky you are.

"Our Table of Organization in this zoo calls for one lion. You are being carried as a monkey."

(FSP.)

● **Ormerod's Rule.** Don't try to think like the top until you are the top.

(David Ormerod, Middletown, Ohio.)

● **Oshry's Laws.** (1) It only snows on sale days. (2) Memorandums say less than memos. Memos say less than picking up a phone. (3) No name, no matter how simple, can be understood correctly over the phone.

(James B. Oshry, Elizabeth, N.J.)

● **O'Toole's Rule.** It is far better to play Hamlet in Denver than to play Laertes in New York.

(Actor Peter O'Toole. *MLS.*)

● **Otten's Revision.** The wages of sin are royalties.
(Jane Otten, in *The Washington Post,* February 12, 1978, *re* Richard Nixon, Wilbur Mills, Margaret Trudeau, etc.)

● **Owens's Law.** All humans will defend, on moral grounds, that which fattens their pocketbooks.

(Gwinn Owens, in *The Baltimore Evening Sun,* May 9, 1979. *ME.*)

● **Oxford Rule.** It's is not, it isn't ain't, and it's it's, not its, if you mean it is. If you don't, it's its. Then too, it's hers. It isn't

her's. It isn't our's either. It's ours, and likewise yours and theirs.
(A very useful rule from Oxford University Press that
appeared in *Edpress News,* April 1979.)

● **Ozard's Rain Rule.** The amount of rain is directly proportional to the length of time your raincoat is at the dry cleaner.
(Bill Ozard, Calgary, Alberta.)

● **Ozian Deception.** Pay no attention to the man behind
the curtain.
(The Wizard of Oz to Dorothy and friends. From Larry
Groebe, San Antonio.)

P

● **Palmer's Law.** The only thing better than a lie is a true story that nobody will believe.
(Joe Palmer.)

● **Pancoast's Periodical Discovery.** The part of a magazine cover that you especially want to see has been covered with the address label.
(Charles Pancoast, Akron, Ohio.)

● **Pangraze's Secret.** PLAN BACKWARD!
(Joe Pangraze, Lynn, Mass.)

● **Paper's Law.** If a museum owns one cuneiform tablet, the likelihood is very high that it will be displayed upside down.
(Herbert H. Paper, Dean, School of Graduate Studies, Hebrew Union College, Cincinnati, from his letter in *The Biblical Archaeology Review,* May/June 1979. Paper adds in a letter to the Center that the law is applicable to any unfamiliar script—for instance, a recent U.S. government poster in which Korean script is displayed upside down.)

● **Pardieck's Laws of Commencement.** (1) The amount of ceremony, pomp, and circumstance involved in a commencement program is in inverse proportion to the level of education. (2) The value of the graduation gift received is in inverse proportion to class rank.
(Robert L. Pardieck, Director of Placement, Bradley University, Peoria.)

● **Parry's Law of Weather Forecasting.** When the weatherman predicts 30 percent chance of rain, rain is twice as likely as when 60 percent chance is predicted.

(J. Thomas Parry, Rockford, Ill.)

● **Parson Weems's Law.** Historical fancy is more persistent than historical fact.

(*American Heritage,* April 1971. A law that explains Washington and the cherry tree, Pilgrims leaping onto Plymouth Rock, Lincoln courting Ann Rutledge, and more.)

● **Parsons's Rule.** At whatever stage you apologize to your spouse, the reply is constant—"It's too late now."

(Denys Parsons, London.)

● **Patton's Law of Sacrifice.** You don't win wars by dying for your country; you win wars by making the other poor bastard die for his country.

(Gen. George Patton, from Joseph A. Horton, M.D., Philadelphia.)

● **Paula Principle.** In a hierarchy women are not allowed to rise to their level of incompetence.

(This discovery was announced in a paper "The Paula Principle and Women's Liberation," by Benjamin Mittman, Evanston, Ill. Mittman examined the Peter Principle ["In a hierarchy every employee tends to rise to his level of incompetence"] and asked the following: "[If] the Peter Principle were universally true, why has not society crashed into the chasm of incompetence? How can institutions, governments, and business survive? What has prevented the Peter Principle from destroying civilization? What mitigating influence has saved us?" The answer is the Paula Principle, which has "sustained society." *RS.*)

● **Paulg's Law.** Remember: In America it's not how much the item costs, it's how much you save.

(Sale ad for Kroch's & Brentano's Bookstores, the *Chicago Tribune,* December 7, 1978.)

● **Pearson's Principle of Organizational Complexity.** The difficulty in running an organization is equal to the square of the number of people divided by the sum of their true applied mentalities.

E.g.: Normal Individual:

$$\frac{1^2}{1} = 1$$

Family of four (one teen, one child):

$$\frac{4^2}{1 + 1 + .5 + .3} = 5.71$$

Government:

$$\frac{Many^2}{13.2} = \infty$$

(Carl M. Pearson, Dallas.)

● **Peary's Preachment.** Many are cold, but few are frozen. (Attributed to the Arctic explorer by Col. William C. Hunter in his *Brass Tacks* [1910].)

● **Peer's Theorem.** The person you're leaving a note for always appears just as you finish writing it.
(Mrs. Clifford R. Peer, Palos Verdes Estates, Cal.)

● **Penner's Principle.** When the math starts to get messy —QUIT!

(*U*/From an unsigned, typewritten paper entitled "Handbuch Für Uplousen das Laboratorywerke und Ubercovern das Grosse Goofups." *TJR.*)

● **Perfection Unmasked.** If your own performance of a job looks perfect to you, it isn't because you've done a perfect job. It's only because you have imperfect standards!

(U/ME.)

● **Perlsweig's Law.** People who can least afford to pay rent, pay rent. People who can most afford to pay rent, build up equity.

(U/DRW.)

● **Peters's Principle of Success.** Get up one time more than you're knocked down.

(Country singer Jimmie Peters, quoted in the *San Antonio Express News,* January 19, 1979.)

● **Peterson's Admonition.** When you think you're going down for the third time—just remember you may have counted wrong.

(Rolfe Peterson, quoted by Bennett Cerf in *The Laugh's on Me,* Doubleday, 1959.)

● **Petroff's 27th Law of Hierarchical Behavior.** Humility decreases with every promotion, and disappears completely at the vice-presidential level. *Corollary:* Arbitrariness increases with every promotion, and becomes absolute at the vice-presidential level.

(John N. Petroff, Dhahran, Saudi Arabia.)

● **Petronius Arbiter's Observation.** We trained hard, but it seemed that every time we were beginning to form up into teams, we would be reorganized. I was to learn later in life that we tend to meet any new situation by reorganizing, and a wonderful method it can be for creating the illusion of progress while only producing confusion, inefficiency, and demoralization.

(Attributed to Petronius Arbiter, Greek naval officer, A.D. 66. From Bob Burkhart.)

● **Philanthropy, First Law of.** It is more blessed to give than to receive, and it's deductible.
(The Wall Street Journal. TCA.)

● **Pi R Rule.**

$$\pi r^2$$

πr^2—Pie are square.
$\pi r^{\prime}$—Pie are not square!
πr^0—Pie are round.
Cr^2—Cornbread are square.
(From Wayne C. Fields, Jr., Newcastle, Cal., who found it on the wall of the library men's room at the California State University, Sacramento.)

● **Pietropinto's Peter Pan Principle.** Marriages peter out or pan out.
(Anthony Pietropinto, M.D., in *Husbands and Wives*, Times Books, 1979.)

● **Pilot's Report.** I am lost but I'm making record time.
(Anonymous pilot somewhere over the Pacific, World War II. Andrew Weissman, New York City.)

● **Pipeline Pete's Observation.** The Lord's Prayer has 56 words; at Gettysburg, Lincoln spoke only 268 long-remembered words; and we got a whole country goin' on the 1,322 words in the Declaration of Independence. So how come it took the federal government 26,911 words to issue a regulation on the sale of cabbages?
(Mobil Corp. ad in *Parade* magazine, April 10, 1977.)

● **Pitt's Hypothesis.** When things go wrong, there are always two faults, the second of which becomes apparent only after the first has been rectified.
(U/*Adhesives Age* magazine, March, 1979. *ME.*)

PITT'S HYPOTHESIS

● **Plato's Distinction.** Man is a two-legged animal without feathers.

(Plato.)

● **Pogo's Dictum.** A long run of good luck is a sure sign of bad luck.

(Pogo. From Michael L. Lazare, Armonk, N.Y.)

● **Poker, Iron Law of.** The winners tell funny stories; the losers cry, "Deal!"

(U/MLS.)

● **Political Law of Nature.** To err is human; to blame it on the other party is politics.

(From *The Light Touch,* edited by Charles Preston, Rand McNally and Co., 1965.)

● **Political Leadership, The First Law of.** Find out where the people want to go, then hustle yourself around in front of them.

(James J. Kilpatrick, in *Nation's Business,* January 1979.)

● **Politico's Law.** No one ever lost an election for a speech he didn't make.

(MLS.)

● **Polsby's Law of Families.** The children of your parents' friends are always nurds.

(Presidential scholar Nelson Polsby. *AO.*)

● **Pop's Law.** Watched boils never pop.

(Paul Seabury, who submitted this law on his stationery from the highly regarded Hoover Institution on War, Revolution, and Peace, Stanford, Cal.)

● **Porter-Givens's Perception.** The delay and expense involved in any action soar in perpendicular proportion to the number of approvals essential to take that action.

> (Columnist Sylvia Porter and Attorney Richard A. Givens, from Porter's August 11, 1978, column.)

● **Porter's Home Rule.** Home is where your garbage is.
> (David Porter. From Ian MacPherson, Regina, Sask.)

● **Poulsen's Law.** When anything is used to its full potential, it will break.
> *(U/DRW.)*

● **Powell's Variation on Murphy's Law.** We have found over and over that if any statement can be screwed up and reported in a way that is disquieting to the public and the economy, it will be screwed up.

> (Jody Powell, quoted in *The Washington Post,* June 6, 1979.)

● **Prentice's Congressional Constant.** There are two periods when Congress does no business: one is before the holidays, and the other after.

> (American journalist and humorist George D. Prentice.)

● **Preudhomme's Law of Window Cleaning.** It's on the other side.
> *(U/DRW.)*

● **Price's Advice.** It's all a game—play it to have fun.
> (C. Kevin Price, Plymouth, Minn.)

● **Price's Rule.** A fool and his money get a lot of attention from headwaiters.

(Roger Price from *In One Head and Out the Other,* Simon and Schuster, 1951.)

● **Procrastination, Laws of.** (1) Procrastination shortens the job and places the responsibility for its termination on someone else (the authority who imposed the deadline). (2) It reduces anxiety by reducing the expected quality of the project from the best of all possible efforts to the best that can be expected given the limited time. (3) Status is gained in the eyes of others, and in one's own eyes, because it is assumed that the importance of the work justifies the stress. (4) Avoidance of interruptions including the assignment of other duties can be achieved, so that the obviously stressed worker can concentrate on the single effort. (5) Procrastination avoids boredom; one never has the feeling that there is nothing important to do. (6) It may eliminate the job if the need passes before the job can be done.
(U/DRW.)

● **Proposal-Writing Rules.** (1) Never mention money. "Resources" is the prime substitute, although "allocations" and "appropriations" are also popular. (2) Fluff up a proposal with the sort of euphemisms that bestow an aura of importance without revealing anything specific.
(Louis Kaplan, planner, quoted in *Newsweek,* May 6, 1968.)

● **Propriis's Bottom Line.** A man should be intelligent enough to wish he were more so.
(U/RA.)

● **Proverbs in Need of Revival.** (1) An emperor may have the measles. (2) The man who breaks his eggs in the center is a fool. (3) Shave with a file, if you like, but don't blame the razor. (4) The hasty man drinks his tea with a fork. (5) New milk is not got from a statue.

(From an old British almanac, quoted in *Comic Almanac* edited by Thomas Yoseloff, A.S. Barnes and Co., 1963.)

● **Public Relations Truism.** There's nothing neither good nor bad that can't be made more so.

(Earle Ferris, public relations counsel, quoted in *The Care and Feeding of Executives* by Millard C. Foeght and Lawrence Hammond, Wormwood Press, 1945.)

● **Putt's Law.** Technology is dominated by two types of people: those who understand what they do not manage, and those who manage what they do not understand.

(Archibald Putt [pseud.], in *Research/Development* magazine, January 1976. *ME.*)

Q

● **Q's Law.** No matter what stage of completion one reaches in a North Sea (oil) field, the cost of the remainder of the project remains the same.

(U/GT.)

● **Quality of Life Constant.** Each time in your life when you think you are about to be able to make both ends meet, somebody moves the ends.

(U/Ra.)

● **Quigley's Laws.** (1) If you take off your right-hand glove in very cold weather, the key will be in your left-hand pocket. (2) Any system that works perfectly will be revised. (3) Backfire hurts only those who get behind things. (4) Courage of conviction results in the conviction of courage.

(Martin Quigley, editor of the *Midwest Motorist. EV.*)

● **Quin's Postulate.** A man must sometimes rise above principle.

(Representative Percy Edwards Quin, Mississippi, 1921.)

● **Quinn's Creed of the Follower.** Lemmings know something we don't.

(A. W. Quinn, Arlington Heights, Ill.)

● **Quirk's Zipper Discovery.** Zippers tend to fail at crucial moments simply because they are treacherous, back-stabbing little fiends.

("Dr. Emory Quirk, the Cleveland Institute of Inanimate

Hostilities," quoted in a column by Dan Myers, the *San Francisco Chronicle*, June 3, 1979.)

● **Quixote's Conclusion.** Facts are the enemy of truth. (Don Quixote, in *Man of La Mancha*. From William C. Young, Ballston Lake, N.Y.)

R

Rabinow's Law. If the top man is no good, all the people below him will be no good in the same way.

(Jacob Rabinow, National Bureau of Standards. *FSP.*)

Radovic's Rule. In any organization, the potential is much greater for the subordinate to manage his superior than for the superior to manage his subordinate.

(Igor Radovic, in *How to Manage the Boss; or, The Radovic Rule,* M. Evans, 1973.)

Rafferty's Laws of Education. (1) Educational research that flies in the teeth of common sense is for the birds. (2) In any election, the candidate supported by the teachers' union is always the one to vote against. (3) Every educational problem is caused by (a) stupidity or (b) unwillingness to work. (4) Fifty percent of all school administrators are superfluous. (5) Sixty percent of the things schools do have nothing to do with education. (6) Any educational area supported by federal funds deteriorates in quality and output in exact proportion to the amount of said federal aid.

(Conservative educator/columnist Max Rafferty. *ME.*)

Ranger's Rule. We have done so much with so little for so long, that now we can do anything with nothing.

(This came from U.S. troops in Vietnam and has been applied widely since.)

Rangnekar's Modified Rules Concerning Decisions. (1) If you must make a decision, delay it. (2) If you can authorize someone else to avoid a decision, do so. (3) If you can form a committee, have them avoid the decision. (4) If you can otherwise avoid a decision, avoid it immediately.

(U/GT.)

● **Ranthony's College Notebook.** (1) A liberal education teaches what is possible. Experience teaches what is not. (2) Songs of the tenured immovable object: (a) I teach to have something to test. I test to have something to grade. (b) Publish the thought or perish the thought. (3) Remember that one advantage of a very good college is that you leave behind the sort of person who functions best in chaos. You will not be at his mercy again unless you are drafted, sent to jail, or teach school. (4) Motto carved over every university's main gate: *Ici e Collegium in mundus bunchum juvenalia de primer stratum passum, et alumni cum cupiditas becommen, Dei Gratia.* (5) Just as starlight seen from Earth shows the stars as they were in the past, so does a university's reputation in the lay community reflect the accomplishments of an earlier time—and for the same reason: distance. (6) The college fraternity is dedicated to the study and celebration of the various liquids and solids that—either naturally or by force —go in and come out of the human body. (7) Two rules of housekeeping: (a) Treat bedsheets like litmus paper: leave them alone until they change color. (b) That part of the room which is within one inch of the floor (three inches beneath the bed) is the province of dust, and the rest is yours. Dust, in return for being granted sanctuary, will stay where it is, not rolling in a big ball out to the middle of the room to beg for pennies and paper clips, embarrassing you in front of guests.

(Ryan Anthony, Tucson.)

● **Ranthony's Observation on Cussing.** The English language has so few cuss words that, much like the flag, they should not be displayed day after day, but kept inside, lovingly rolled up and stored away, to bring forth proudly, unfaded, and effective on special occasions.

(Ryan Anthony, Tucson.)

● **Raper's Rules.** (1) Hit the ball over the fence and you can take your time going around the bases. (2) Don't claim too much. The manufacturer of hair restorer never advertises that it will grow hair on the back of the neck. (3) The proof of the pudding is in the demand for it. (4) Patience is fine, but it never helped a rooster lay an agg.

(John W. Raper, in *What This World Needs,* World, 1945.)

● **Raymond's Rule on Junk Mail.** If it doesn't look as if there is a check or a personal letter in it, there's nothing in it—so throw it out.

(Columnist John Raymond, *The Atlanta Constitution,* March 13, 1979.)

● **Reasons Why Not (50 Handy-Dandy Excuses).** (1) We've never done it before. (2) Nobody else has ever done it. (3) It has never been tried before. (4) We tried it before. (5) Another company (person) tried it before. (6) We've been doing it this way for 25 years. (7) It won't work in a small company. (8) It won't work in a large company. (9) It won't work in our company. (10) Why change—it's working OK. (11) The boss will never buy it. (12) It needs further investigation. (13) Our competitors are not doing it. (14) It's too much trouble to change. (15) Our company is different. (16) The ad dept. says it can't be done. (17) The sales dept. says it can't be sold. (18) The service dept. won't like it. (19) The janitor says it can't be done. (20) It can't be done. (21) We don't have the money. (22) We don't have the personnel. (23) We don't have the equipment. (24) The union will scream. (25) It's too visionary. (26) You can't teach an old dog new tricks. (27) It's too radical a change. (28) It's beyond my responsibility. (29) It's not my job. (30) We don't have the time.

(31) It will obsolete other procedures. (32) Customers won't buy it. (33) It's contrary to policy. (34) It will increase overhead. (35) The employees will never buy it. (36) It's not our problem. (37) I don't like it. (38) You're right, but . . . (39) We're not ready for it. (40) It needs more thought. (41) Management won't accept it. (42) We can't take the chance. (43) We'd lose money on it. (44) It takes too long to pay out. (45) We're doing all right as it is. (46) It needs committee study. (47) Competition won't like it. (48) It needs sleeping on. (49) It won't work in this department. (50) It's impossible.

> (This list has been popular in engineering circles for years. The earliest published appearance was in *Product Engineering,* July 20, 1959. It was supplied to the magazine by E. F. Borisch of the Milwaukee Gear Co.)

● **Reik's Razor.** If you see a snake coming toward you in a jungle, you have a right to be anxious; if you see it coming down Park Avenue, you're in trouble.

> (Theodore Reik.)

● **Reis's Law of Airplane Travel.** Whatever airline you fly and whatever airport you fly to, you always land at Gate 102.
> (Harold Reis. *AO.*)

● **Remusat's Reconciliation.** (1) You must pay for your sins. (2) If you've already paid, please disregard this notice.
> (Jeanne Remusat, Forest Hills, N.Y. This appeared originally in a "New York Magazine Competition," *New York,* November 28, 1977.)

● **Repartee, First Rule of.** Better never than late.
> *(U/Ra.)*

● **Retsof's Rush Hour Blizzard Law.** If there is a suitable morning snowstorm, an employee will leave after the storm to go to work. Given an equivalent afternoon snowstorm, the employee will leave before the storm to go home.

(John C. Foster, Columbus, Ohio. For reasons unclear, Foster spells his name backward when composing laws.)

Special Section 15

Revised Proverbs. Nothing hangs on quite like an old proverb, which is one reason they require occasional scrapping and updating. The list of those that should be abandoned is long—starting with such inanities as:

—A picture is worth a thousand words. (Leo Rosten has rebutted this with, "OK. Draw me a picture of the Gettysburg Address.")

—Handsome is as handsome does. (A notion that is wrong-headed beyond belief.)

—You can't make a silk purse out of a sow's ear. (First of all, who would want to. Secondly, some years ago a Boston research firm actually made such a purse distilling a silky substance from a pot of sow's ears.)

—As for revisions the possibilities are limitless. For instance, all of these collected updates of one old saw are more to the point than the original:

—A fool and his money are some party.

—A fool and his money are soon spotted.

—A fool and his money are soon mated.

—A fool and his money are invited everywhere.

—A fool and his money are the prime-time television target audience. *(MLS.)*

—A Pool. And your money is soon parted.

In no special order, here are some other relevant revisions:
—Many hands want light work.
—The early worm, on the other hand, gets eaten by the bird.
—If you give a man enough rope, he'll hang you.
—Perversity makes for strange bedfellows.
—The wages of sin vary considerably.
—A word to the wise is superfluous.
—Counting your chickens before they've hatched is sensible long-range planning.
—Familiarity breeds.
—People who live in stone houses shouldn't throw glasses.
—Early to bed and early to rise and you'll be groggy when everyone else is alert.
—Out of the mouths of babes comes Gerber's strained apricots.
—Every silver lining has its cloud.
—If at first you don't succeed, you've got one strike against you.
—A bird in the hand is inconvenient.
—Lots of Jack makes all work play.
—A milligram of prevention is worth a kilogram of cure.
—A rolling stone angers his boss.
—Poets are born not paid.
—Some are born great, some achieve greatness, and some have a great thirst upon them.
—He who hesitates is bossed.

● **Revisionist's Rule.** The easiest way to change history is to become a historian.

(Unattributed quote, NASA file.)

● **Rhodes's Law.** When any principle, law, tenet, probability, happening, circumstance, or result can in no way be directly, indirectly, empirically, or circuitously proven, derived, implied, inferred, induced, deducted, estimated, or scientifically guessed, it will always for the purpose of convenience, expediency, political advantage, material gain, or personal comfort, or any combination of the above, or none of the above, be unilaterally and unequivocally assumed, proclaimed, and adhered to as absolute truth to be undeniably, universally, immutably, and infinitely so, until such time as it becomes advantageous to assume otherwise, maybe. (The full impact of this fundamental law may be invoked by use of the following symbolic logical operator, commonly referred to as "Charlie's Loop":

(Charles E. Rhodes, Allison Park, Penn. Rhodes, who has been working on his law for some time, states that the original discovery was made c. 1971 in its original, less scientific form: "When in doubt, fake it.")

● **Rice's Rule.**
No matter when you turn on the TV, there is *always* an ad showing.
(Edith K. Rice, East Boothbay, Maine.)

● **Rigsbee's Law of Priorities.** Given the choice between doing something for which one is well-prepared and paid, or doing something for which one is ill-prepared and not paid, most individuals will choose the latter.
(Ken Rigsbee, Bartlesville, Okla. His proof for this law: "I have just written you this letter on company time.")

● **Rigsbee's Principle of Management.** Your brightest, sharpest new employees are the first to leave your organization —as the cream rises to the top it will be skimmed off.
(Ken Rigsbee, again.)

● **Rizzo's Reassurance.** The streets are safe in Philadelphia, it's only the people who make them unsafe.

(Philadelphia Mayor Frank Rizzo.)

● **Robbins's Law of Student Enrollment.** In required courses, failures create their own demand.

(Stephen P. Robbins, Professor, Department of Management, Concordia University, Montreal.)

● **Robert's Paradox.** My teacher says strangers are people we don't know. But that can't be true, because there are people who don't know us and we're not strangers.

(Robert, son of Arnold R. Isaacs, cited in Arnold's "The Rules of the Game" in *The Baltimore Sun,* December 31, 1978.)

● **Robert's Rules of Home and Garden.** (1) If at first you don't succeed, hire a contractor. (2) Two plus two equals four—unless you're talking about inches in a two-by-four. (3) Mulch is ado about nothing. (4) An idle mind should not mess around in a power workshop. (5) We must all hang together or assuredly the pictures will be crooked. (6) Somebody said it couldn't be done. I'll go along with that.

(Bob Herguth, the *Chicago Sun-Times. RS.*)

● **Robertson's Rules of Lunch.** (1) If it isn't deductible, don't. (2) There are no free lunches, but usually the IRS will pay for a part. (3) Everyone has to eat. (4) When there are no other ways to minimize the cost of the meal, most diners try to stiff the waiter.

(James A. Robertson, El Paso, Tex.)

● **Rochester's Theorem.** Before I got married I had six theories about bringing up children; now I have six children and no theories.

(Lord Rochester.)

● **Rogers's Advice.** Think like a hare, but act like a turtle. (Kenneth J. Rogers, Pontiac, Mich.)

● **Rogers's Sure-fire Formula.** The best way to make a fire with two sticks is to make sure one of them is a match.
(Will Rogers.)

● **Rosa's Buzz-off Theory.** After completing that memo or report, substitute each buzz word with an everyday word. All on distribution will feel self-congratulatory at having for once understood a piece of writing in total. You will make friends.
(Sal Rosa, New York City, who also discovered the next item.)

● **Rosa's Good Lord Willing Law.** If all causes of mishaps are insured against except "Acts of God," the good Lord will invariably oblige.

● **Rosalynn's Rule.** Don't worry about polls—but if you do, don't admit it.
(Rosalynn Carter, quoted by Donnie Radcliffe in *The Washington Post,* October 5, 1978.)

● **Rose's First Law of Investments.** One should never invest in anything that must be painted or fed.
(Showman Billy Rose, from William M. Mills, Hutchinson, Kans.)

● **Rosenblatt's Laws.** (1) The duration of a modern marriage is in direct proportion to the distance from one's relatives. (2) A basic law of modern education states that the further east one's university, the more honored he is the further west he travels. (3) A politician who doesn't swear at all is either an imposter or under indictment.
(Roger Rosenblatt, from his columns for *The Washington Post.*)

● **Rover's Law.** A dog always wants to be on the other side of the door.

   (U/Ra.)

● **Royal's Rule.** Think lucky. If you fall in a pond, check your hip pockets for fish.

   (University of Texas football coach Darrell Royal.)

● **Rubin's Reminder.** Never confuse brilliance with a bull market.

   (Paul Rubin, Toldeo, Ohio.)

● **Rubman's Law.** You always find something the first place you look the second time.

   (Barbara Solonche, who named it for a relative who has proven the law.)

● **Ruby's Principles on Close Encounters.** The probability of meeting someone you know increases when you're with someone you don't want to be seen with.

   (Walter Busch, St. Louis. *EV.*)

● **Ruination, Three Rules of.** There are three ways to be ruined in this world: first is by sex, second is by gambling, and the third is by engineers. Sex is the most fun, gambling is the most exciting, and engineers are the surest.

   (U/ Commonly found printed on cards passed out at engineering conferences.)

● **Russell's Classroom Rules.** (1) No working not permitted. (2) The tardy student will always want to leave early. (3) The size of the grade marked on a paper will be inverse to its importance (small A's and large F's).

   (Gene H. Russell, Director, The Emperor Norton Society, Orland, Cal.)

● **Russell's Rule of Industrial Genetics.** The darker your skin pigmentation, the nearer you sit to the front window.

(Jim Russell, from his book *Russell on Murphy's Law,* Celestial Arts, 1978, as is the next item.)

● **Russell's Seismological Discovery.** Everything east of the San Andreas Fault will eventually plunge into the Atlantic Ocean.

● **Rutherford's Rule.** The more you don't know how to do, the less you have to do.

(Larry Rutherford, Virginia Military Institute.)

ROSE'S FIRST LAW OF INVESTMENTS

S

● **Sachar's Observation.** Some people grow with responsibility—others merely swell.

> (Abram Sachar, Chancellor of Brandeis University. From Richard S. Luskin, Needham, Mass.)

● **Safire's New Law of Who/Whom in Headlines.** When "whom" is correct, use some other formulation.

> (William Safire, *The New York Times Magazine,* March 25, 1979. From Rabbi Wayne Allen, Staten Island, N.Y.)

● **Sally's Law of Beauty.** In any given beauty salon, the total beauty of the operators exceeds that of the customers by a factor of 4:1. The sex of the operators and customers is immaterial.

> (N. Sally Hass, Sleepy Hollow, Ill.)

● **Sally's Rule of Aquatic Relativity.** The neatest thing that can happen to a girl at the pool is to have two guys take her hands and feet and throw her into the water, unless the two guys are her brothers, in which case it is the worst thing that can happen to a girl.

> (Sally, a teen-ager known to Michael L. Lazare, Armonk, N.Y.)

● **Samuelson's Corollary.** Public bureaucracy breeds private bureaucracy.

> (Robert J. Samuelson, *The Washington Post,* June 6, 1978. As he explains, "The more government expands, the more it stimulates a vast supporting apparatus of trade

associations, lawyers, lobbyists, research groups, econo-
mists, and consultants—all trying to shape the direction
of new federal regulations and spending programs.")

● **Sanders's Law.** You never get walked on unless you
throw yourself on the floor.
(Chicago radio personality Betty Sanders.)

● **Sandy's Theory.** Depression and lack of inspiration are
in equal proportion to the lack of involvement and inspiration.
(Ellie Saraquese, Carmichael, Cal.)

● **Sans Souci Rule.** You are where you eat.
(Named for the Washington restaurant of the same name.
The rule was given to Art Buchwald by Pierre Salinger
when Buchwald first arrived in Washington.)

● **Santayana's Philosophical Reminder.** It is a great advantage for a system of philosophy to be substantially true.
(George Santayana.)

● **Sartorial Homogeneity, The Law of.** If you are called on
to speak at a gathering of your superiors and you are wearing
brown, everyone else is wearing blue. If you are wearing blue,
everyone else is wearing gray.
(Michael L. Lazare, Armonk, N.Y., from his own empirical studies.)

● **Schapiro's Logical Explanation.** The grass is always
greener on the other side, but that is only because they use more
manure.
(Ken Schapiro, Montclair, N.J.)

● **Scheussler's Rule of Four.** In a group of four people, one will always be honest, one will always be crooked, and the other two must be watched.

(R. W. Scheussler, Pittsburgh, Penn.)

● **Schinto-Bacal's Four Steps to Becoming a Legend in Your Time.** (1) Start a fad or religion. (2) Charm birds off trees. (3) Build an empire. (4) Never volunteer.

(Gene Schinto and Jules Bacal from their book *How to Become a Legend in Your Own Lifetime,* Abelard-Schuman, 1966.)

● **Schlegel's Two-Student Theory.** Of two students, one will begin immediately working on a difficult problem set (or other homework) while the other fools around. The night before the homework is due, the "fooler" will seek out the "worker" and will want to find out how to do the problems. The "fooler" will then: (1) Gleefully point out all the errors in the "worker's" solution; (2) Get a better grade on the homework.

(Eric M. Schlegel, Bloomington, Ind.)

● **Schonfeld's Law of Cameras.** The best shots occur: (1) When you are out of film; (2) when you don't have your camera; (3) when you are looking the other way.

(Jerry Schonfeld, Portsmouth, Va.)

● **Schorr's Laws of Economics.** (1) If there are imperfections in the structure of the marketplace, entrepreneurs will make lots of money. (2) If there are no imperfections in the structure of the marketplace, entrepreneurs will make imperfections in the structure of the marketplace.

(Kenneth L. Schorr, Little Rock, Ark.)

● **Schroeder's Admonition.** Don't ask questions you don't want answers to.

(Capt. Schroeder, USCG, from W. R. Jurgens, Bowie, Md.)

S
—
200

SCHONFELD'S LAW OF CAMERAS

● **Schulze's Restatement.** Always stop along the way to smell the roses—your competitors will be happy to get you out of their way.

(Paul Schulze III, Chicago.)

● **Schwartz's True View of Life.** Don't look for your real success until you're past fifty. It takes that long to get over the distractions of sex.

(Eddie Schwartz of Minneapolis, quoted in *A Couple of Cards* by Alfred McVay and Ed Hickey Associated Marketing Enterprises, 1973.)

● **Schwemer's Pontification.** The number of variables required to define completely a system or process will always exceed by one the number of experiments performed, regardless of the number of experiments performed.

(Warren Schwemer, Ashland, Ky.)

● **Science, Basic Definitions.** (1) If it's green or wiggles, it's biology. (2) If it stinks, it's chemistry. (3) If it doesn't work, it's physics.

(U/TJR.)

● **Scott's Do-It-Yourself Code.** (1) Any tool left on top of a ladder will fall off and hit you in the head. (2) Any rope left dragging from any object in any location will catch on something. (3) For the successful completion of any task requiring tools, it is necessary to bleed at least once.

(Bill Scott, Tujunga, Cal.)

● **Scott's Hypothesis.** If it doesn't play in Peoria—it probably will in Dubuque.

(Sid Scott, former Peoria resident, now living in Dubuque.)

● **Seligson-Gerberg-Corman Rule of Sexual Sameness.** Having bad sex with someone you care about is the same as having bad sex with someone you don't care about.

(Marcia Seligson, Mort Gerberg, and Avery Corman, from their book, *The Everything in the World That's the Same as Something Else Book,* Simon and Schuster, 1969.)

● **Sgt. Preston's Law of the Wild.** The scenery only changes for the lead dog.

(Curt Heinfelden, Baltimore.)

● **Shanebrook's Law.** If you do a job twice, it's yours.

(J. Richard Shanebrook, Chairman, Mechanical Engineering Department, Union College, Schenectady, N.Y.)

● **Shannon's Law.** Nothing is simple.

(Stan Shannon, Dallas.)

● **Shannon's Observation.** Nothing is so frustrating as a bad situation that is beginning to improve.

(William V. Shannon. *ME.*)

● **Shapiro/Kaufman Law.** The lag in American productivity is directly related to the steady increase in the number of business conferences and conventions.

(Walter Shapiro and Aleta Kaufman in their article "Conferences and Conventions: the $20-Billion Industry That Keeps America from Working." *The Washington Monthly,* February 1977.)

● **Sharples's Philosophy.** (1) A rolling stone gathers momentum. (2) Progress is nondirectional. (3) Don't be taken by the vitamin itself.

(Virginia M. Sharples, Houston.)

● **Shaw's Axiom.** For every problem science solves, it creates ten new ones.
(George Bernard Shaw, from Sydney J. Harris.)

● **Shaw's Golden Rule.** Do not do unto others as you would that they should do unto you; their tastes may be different.
(George Bernard Shaw, quoted by Joseph Wood Krutch in his essay "The Best of Two Worlds." *RS.*)

● **Sheehan's Law of Rational Government.** Using logic to deal with government is illogical; using illogic to deal with government is logical.
(Raymond J. Sheehan, Springfield, Mass.)

● **Shelton's Law of Bill Paying.** The bill was due before you got it.
(John Shelton.)

● **Sheppard's Laws of Organization.** (1) If a surface is flat, pile things on it. (2) If a pile grows to more than one foot tall, start a new pile.
(Jeffrey Sheppard, in *The Washington Post,* January 5, 1979.)

● **Shick's Problematic Laws.** (1) Small problems have deep roots (a zero variance normally indicates that errors of + 1000 and −1000 have occurred simultaneously and canceled one another.) (2) Large problems are the cause of small problems (an error in judgment in the beginning brings on an awful lot of judgment for error in the end). (3) There is no problem a good miracle can't solve.
(Harry R. Shick, San Bernardino, Cal.)

● **Shields's Eternal Questions.** (1) How does Yassir Arafat constantly maintain a two-day growth of beard? (2) Who does

Anita Bryant's hair? (3) Why does Menachem Begin always look like he's eaten a bad meal?

> (Political consultant Mark Shields, who asked these on his WRC radio show.)

● **Shore's Absolute Law.** Any unexpected and undesirable negative quantities or results may be rectified by the judicious insertion of absolute-value signs and prayerful interjections (e.g. ''Dammit!'').

> (U/from Warren Schwemer, Ashland, Ky.)

● **Short's Quotations (A New Selection).** (1) The hardest lesson to learn is that learning is a continual process. (2) The only thing worse than learning the truth is not learning the truth. (3) The human brain is the only computer in the world made out of meat. (4) A human being is a computer's way of building another computer: usually a better one. That's why computers will never decide to replace human beings. We are their sex organs. (5) One fact can change your whole point of view. For instance, did you know King Kong was a lesbian? (6) If the opposite of *pro* is *con,* then what is the opposite of progress? (7) The more you treasure the object, the more noticeable the flaw. (8) Even Murphy's Law goes wrong sometimes.

> (David Gerrold, a.k.a. Solomon Short, from his work in progress *Quotebook of Solomon Short.* See also *Gerrold's Law.*)

● **Sieger's Law.** You will have the same amount of money left at the end of the month, no matter how many raises, bonuses, or windfalls occur during the month.

> (U/Ra.)

● **Sign at the Pentagon.**
THEY TOLD HIM THE JOB COULDN'T BE DONE.
HE ROLLED UP HIS SLEEVES AND WENT TO IT.

HE TACKLED THE JOB THAT COULDN'T BE DONE
—AND HE COULDN'T DO IT.
(*U/* Department of Defense.)

● **Sissman's First Twenty Rules of Reviewing.** Never review the work of a friend.

(Critic L. E. Sissman, quoted by Johnathan Yardley in *The
Washington Star,* March 11, 1979. *JCG.*)

● **Sit, Whittle, and Spit Club Rules.** (1) Don't sit in the
sun. (2) Don't whittle toward yourself. (3) Don't spit against the
wind.

(Reported by Clyde W. Wilkinson, in his article "Back-
woods Humor" in the *Southwest Review,* January
1939.)

● **Skinnell's Rule.** You don't start traditions, traditions start.
(K. W. Skinnell, Bethel Park, Penn.)

● **Skinner's Law.** Anyone who owns a telephone is at the
mercy of any damn fool who knows how to dial.

(Jean Skinner Ostlund, Willmar, Minn., who learned it
from her father, the late Arthur Z. Skinner.)

● **Sklenar's Second Rule.** No time is a convenient time for
a meeting.

(Leslie James Sklenar, Chicago.)

● **Skole's Hotel Law.** When, through hard work, chance,
position, or other fortuitous circumstances, you finally can stay
in a hotel you could only dream of in your youth, it has deteri-
orated into a dump.

(Bob Skole, Stockholm, Sweden, written on the stationery
of a famous New York hotel.)

● **Slavens's Discoveries.** (1) The toilet paper never runs out on the other guy. (2) Never let a drunk friend drive—especially if the party was at *his* place. (3) People with strong minds have weak eyes. (4) A good newspaper column cannot be written unless there is a can of beer on one side of the typewriter and a bag of Doritos on the other.

(Larry M. Slavens, Publisher, *The Fontanelle Observer,* Fontanelle, Iowa.)

● **Slim's Law.** Any significant military action will occur at the junction of two or more map sheets.

(Field Marshal Viscount Slim of Burma. Richard J. Keogh, Honolulu.)

● **Smith's Fourth Law of Inertia.** A body at rest tends to watch television.

(G. Guy Smith, Media, Penn.)

● **Smith-Johannsen's Secret of Longevity.** Stay busy, get plenty of exercise, and don't drink too much. Then again, don't drink too little.

(Herman "Jackrabbit" Smith-Johannsen, 103-year-old Canadian cross-country skier, quoted in *Sports Illustrated,* August 21, 1978.)

● **Smith's Laws.** *Small Appliance Axiom:* If it doesn't break immediately it can never be fixed. *2d Small Appliance Axiom:* If it breaks immediately, by the time it's fixed it will be too late to fix it if it breaks again. *Marketing:* You can never buy the new improved version because a new improved version is already replacing it.

(Jerry Smith, Florissant, Mo.)

● **Smith's Observation.** There is nothing so trivial, so esoteric, so unique, or so commonplace, but someone will spend time and effort in an attempt to codify it.

(John Stephen Smith, Lincoln, Neb.)

● **Smith's Writing Rule.** In composing, as a general rule, run your pen through every other word you have written; you have no idea what vigor it will give your style.

(English clergyman and essayist Sydney Smith, 1771–1845.)

● **Smock's Travel Observations.** (1) Every country is a "land of contrast." (2) Wherever you travel, the weather is "unusual for this time of year."

(Ruth J. Smock, Silver Spring, Md.)

● **Smolik's Law.** Anything highly publicized needs to be.
(Richard C. Smolik, St. Louis.)

● **SNAFU Principle.** Communication is only possible between equals.

(From *Illuminatus* by Robert Shea and Robert Anson Wilson. From John W. Gustafson, Chicago.)

● **Socio-Genetics, Second Law of.** The law of heredity is that all undesirable traits come from the other parent.

("Morning Smile" column, *The Toronto Globe and Mail,* February 21, 1979. From Richard Isaac, M.D., Toronto.)

● **Solis's Amendment.** There is no such thing as a free lunch . . . the lunch gets more expensive each year.

(L. L. Solis, Columbus, Ohio. Letter to *The Wall Street Journal,* November 11, 1974.)

● **Somary's Fifteenth Law.** The less protection the State provides for its citizens, the more it charges for the job.

(Swiss banker Felix Somary; one of his twenty social laws from *Crisis and the Future of Democracy.* Quoted by Brian Crozier in *The National Review,* March 1979. *JCG.*)

● **Spaatz's Three Rules for the Conduct of Air Force Officers Before Congressional Committees.** (1) Don't try to be funny. (2) Don't lie. (3) Don't blurt out the truth.
(Gen. Tooey Spaatz, Chief of Staff, USAF, from Brig. Gen. William J. Becker, USAF.)

● **Spats's Restatement.** Every silver lining has a cloud.
(The character "Spats" Baxter in *Movie Movie.*)

● **Speculating on Margin, Three Good Rules for.** (1) Don't! (2) Do not! (3) If, after careful perusal of the two forementioned Rules, you are still resolved upon Folly, go to your Bank, Cracked Teapot, Old Stocking, or other financial depository where your hard-earned Cash is kept, and, having therefrom taken One Thousand Dollars . . . roll them carefully in strong, brown wrapping-paper and seal the ends. You are now ready for the next step. Placing the Roll in your inside vest pocket proceed briskly to the nearest Ferry slip and take the first boat which leaves. When midway between the termini, walk to the stern of the boat, take out the Roll, and heave it far into the troubled waters. Your money will have then arrived at its terminus, and you should calmly proceed to yours. By following this method of Deposit for your Margin, you not only save Brokers' commission and Interest, but many anxious days and sleepless nights, besides having anticipated by a few hours the Sinking of your Money.
(Gideon Wurdz [Charles Wayland Towne] in *Foolish Finance* [1905].)

● **Spindel's Motivator.** Aim at nothing and you will hit it.
(Donald T. Spindel, St. Louis.)

● **Stanley's Rules of the Road.** (1) The later you are, the greater the length of the red light. (2) The least-traveled roads have the longest green lights.

(Randall L. Stanley, St. Charles, Mo. *EV.*)

● **State Service Syndrome.** Never ask a business question during lunch hour.

(James Brown, former state employee. From Gary Knowlton, Portland, Ore.)

● **Steckel's Rule to Success.** Good enough isn't good enough.

(Paul W. Steckel, Gainesville, Fla.)

● **Steele's Fifth Law of Water Beds.** Bodies tend to oscillate at the same rate that they accelerate.

(Ashley H. Steele, Toledo, Ohio.)

● **Steele's Law of Excellence.** Only 10 percent of anything can be in the top 10 percent.

(Guy L. Steele Jr., Cambridge, Mass.)

● **Stengel's Law.** Good pitching will always stop good hitting and vice versa.

(Casey Stengel. From Steven D. Mirsky, Ithaca, N.Y.)

● **Stephen's Law of Averages.** Based on the summation of parts, divided by the number of samples, the *average* human has one breast and one testicle.

(Stephen J. Grollman, Hartsdale, N.Y.)

● **Stevenson's Presidential Paradox.** By the time a man is nominated for the Presidency of the United States, he is no longer worthy to hold the office.

(Adlai Stevenson, 1956, from Sydney J. Harris.)

● **Stock's Observation.** You no sooner get your head above water than someone pulls your flippers off.
(U/DRW.)

● **Strout's Law.** There is a major scandal in American political life every 50 years: Grant's in 1873, Teapot Dome in 1923, Watergate in 1973. Nail down your seats for 2023.
(Richard Strout, quoted in *Time,* March 27, 1978.)

● **Stults's Situation Report.** Our problems are mostly behind us—what we have to do now is fight the solutions.
(Banker Alan P. Stults, quoted in the *Chicago Tribune,* July 11, 1975.)

● **Sukhomlinov Effect, The.** In war, victory goes to those armies whose leaders' uniforms are least impressive.
(Roger A. Beaumont and Bernard J. James, *Horizon* magazine, Winter 1971.)

● **Sullivan's Law.** All great organizations were built on the backs of blind mules on treadmills. *Corollary:* No great organization was ever built with one-eyed mules.
(J. M. Sullivan, Creve Coeur, Mo.)

● **Sullivan's Proverbial Discovery.** Proverbs usually read just as well backwards, or jumbled up. Fine words do not a parsnip make nor iron bars a summer.
(Humorist Frank Sullivan, from his essay "It's Easy to Quote a Proper Proverb.")

● **Swartz's Maxim.** Live every day as if it were your last . . . and some day you'll be right.
(U/Ra.)

● **Sweeney's Laws.** (1) The joy that is felt at the sight of a new-fallen snow is inversely proportional to the age of the beholder. (2) Today's society will ignore almost any form of public behavior except getting in the express line with two extra items. (3) Never trust a skinny cook.

> (Paul Sweeney, in *The Quarterly,* which he writes for the Defense Mapping Federal Credit Union.)

● **Swinehart's Definition.** The lecture is that procedure whereby the material in the notes of the professor is transferred to the notes of the students without passing through the mind of either.

> (Donald F. Swinehart, Department of Chemistry, University of Oregon. *T/R.*)

● **Sybert's Law of the Workshop.** Whenever a project is undertaken, the least expensive but most important item for its completion will be forgotten (i.e. sandpaper, paintbrushes, etc.).

> (Christopher Sybert, Lutherville, Md.)

● **Szymcik's Universal Law of Experts.** An expert is not someone who is often right, as opposed to a nonexpert; each is wrong about the same percent of the time. But the expert can always tell you why he was wrong; so you can always tell the difference.

> (Rev. Mark Szymcik, Leominster, Mass.)

● **T. Camille's Axioms.** (1) You are always doing something marginal when your boss drops by your desk. (2) You've made a decision whether or not you decided. (3) Title distinctions are functions of everything they shouldn't be. (4) It is easier to do it the hard way. (5) You'd always rather be doing something else when you are doing what you thought you wanted to do. (6) The least important and the most important information gets passed on at the office copying machine. (7) If you haven't asked yourself "Why the hell did I go to college anyway?" you must be teaching. (8) You haven't not worked until you've worked for the government. (9) He's not smarter than you—he's just more convincing. (10) If you feel incompetent, you probably are. (11) If someone else's clout depends on your productivity, (s)/he'll be on your back. (12) I'll do it Monday. (13) May the odds be with you! (14) Nobody likes a smart-ass; nobody likes a dumb-ass either.

(T. Camille Flowers, Cincinnati, Ohio.)

● **Tansik's Law of Bureaucratic Success.** Success in a bureaucracy depends not so much on whom you please, but on whom you avoid making angry. *Corollary:* To succeed, concentrate not on doing great things but on the avoidance of making mistakes.

(David A. Tansik, Associate Professor, University of Arizona.)

● **Taranto's Theorem.** The amount of intelligence on Earth is finite; the population increases exponentially.

(Harri V. Taranto, New York City.)

T. CAMILLE'S AXIOM NO. 1

● **Tatman's Assumption.** Always assume that your assumption is invalid.

   (Robert F. Tatman, Wynnewood, Penn.)

● **Taylor's Discovery.** In any organization there are only two people to contact if you want results—the person at the very top and the person at the very bottom.

   (Warren E. Taylor, Burlington, N.C.)

● **Tennis Players' Ten Commandments.** *I.* Thou shalt have no sport other than tennis. *II.* Thou shalt remember thine appointed court time and put nothing before it. *III.* Thou shalt honor thy backhand as instructed by thy pro. *IV.* Thou shalt not bear false witness as to when thou wast last the provider of new tennis balls. *V.* Thou shalt not take the name of the Lord in vain when thy shot hitteth the tape and faileth to roll over. *VI.* Thou shalt not destroy thy racquet after having lobbed directly to thine opponent at the net. *VII.* Thou shalt not commit a double fault at set point. *VIII.* Thou shalt not steal thy partner's overhead smash. *IX.* Thou shalt not covet they neighbor's court time, nor his or her partner. *X.* Thou shalt not use four-letter expletives when thou hast caused an easy volley to be ensnared in the net.

   (U/NDB.)

Special Section 16

Tests and Examinations

(1) *M.I.T. Graduate Qualifying Examination.*

Instructions: Read each question thoroughly. Answer all questions. Time limit—four hours. Begin immediately.

History. Describe the history of the papacy from its origins to the present day; concentrate specially but not exclusively on the social, political, economic, religious, and philosophical impact on Europe, Asia, America, and Africa. Be brief, concise, and specific.

Medicine. You have been provided with a razor blade, a piece of gauze, and a bottle of Scotch. Remove your own appendix. Do not suture until your work has been inspected. You have fifteen minutes.

Public Speaking. 2,500 riot-crazed aborigines are storming the classroom. Calm them. You may use any ancient language except Latin or Greek.

Biology. Create life. Estimate the differences in subsequent human culture if this form of life had developed 500 million years earlier, with special attention to the probable effects on the English parliamentary system. Prove your thesis.

Music. Write a piano concerto. Orchestrate it and perform it with flute and drum. You will find a piano under your seat.

Psychology. Based on your knowledge of their works, evaluate the emotional stability, degree of adjustment, and repressed frustrations of each of the following: Alexander of Aphrodisias, Ramses II, Hammurabi. Support your evaluation with quotations from each man's work, making appropriate references. It is not necessary to translate.

Sociology. Estimate the sociological problems that might accompany the end of the world. Construct an experiment to test your theory.

Management Science. Define management. Define science. How do they relate? Why? Create a generalized algorithm to optimize all managerial decisions. Assuming an 1130 CPU supporting 50 terminals, each terminal to activate your algorithm, design the communications interface and all the necessary control programs.

Economics. Develop a realistic plan for refinancing the national debt. Trace the possible effects of your plan in the following areas: Cubism, the Donatist controversy, the wave theory of light. Outline a method from all points of view. Point out the deficiencies in your point of view, as demonstrated in your answer to the last question.

Political Science. There is a red telephone on the desk beside you. Start World War III. Report at length on its socio-political effects, if any.

Epistemology. Take a position for or against the truth. Prove the validity of your position.

Physics. Explain the nature of matter. Include in your answer an evaluation of the impact of the development of mathematics on science.

Philosophy. Sketch the development of human thought; estimate its significance. Compare with the development of any other kind of thought.

General Knowledge. Describe in detail. Be objective and specific.

    (U/ME.)

② *North Dakota Null-Hypothesis Inventory. NDNI.*
Instructions: Respond to each statement with one of these three answers: (1) Sometimes; (2) Always; (3) Never.
    1. I salivate at the sight of mittens.
    2. At times I am afraid my toes will fall off.

3. Chopped liver makes me laugh.
4. As an infant, I had very few hobbies.
5. Some people never look at me.
6. I sometimes feel that my earlobes are longer than those of other people.
7. Spinach makes me feel alone.
8. My sex life is A-okay.
9. I often fart in crowds.
10. Dirty stories make me think about sex.
11. I am anxious in rooms that have hairy walls.
12. Cousins are not to be trusted.
13. Sometimes I think someone is trying to take over my stomach.
14. I have never eaten a fly.
15. I cannot read or write.
16. As an infant I hated chopped liver.
17. I have killed mosquitos.
18. My teeth sometimes leave my body.
19. I am never startled by a fish.
20. Plaid Stamps are better than Green Stamps.
21. I have never gone to pieces over the weekend.
22. My parents always faced catastrophe with a song.
23. Recently, I have been getting shorter.
24. I have taken shoe polish to excess.
25. I have always been disturbed by the size of Lincoln's ears.
26. Chicken liver gives me a rash.
27. I like mannish children.
28. Most of the time I go to sleep without saying good-bye.
29. I am not afraid of picking up door knobs.
30. Chiclets make me sweat.
31. I stay in the bathtub until I look like a raisin.
32. Frantic screams make me nervous.
33. It makes me angry to have people bury me.
34. I hate orgies, if nobody else is there.
35. I am afraid of Vikings.

(Shortened version of a longer NDNI. The NDNI is another classic of unknown origin that the author first came in contact with in 1964 in New York. It is, of course, a replacement for the ubiquitous Minnesota Multiphasic Personality Inventory [MMPI], which is used to create data for everyone ranging from college administrators to prison wardens. There is now an even newer test called the "No-Nonsense Personality Inventory," published for the first time in the November 1978 issue of *The Journal of Irreproducible Results,* which asks for response to such statements as: "I am often bothered by thoughts of sex while having intercourse," "God rarely answers my questions," "Weeping brings tears to my eyes," and "I often bite other people's nails.")

③ *Test Entitled "Can you follow directions?" (three-minute time test).*

1. Read everything before doing anything.
2. Put your name in the upper right-hand corner of this paper.
3. Circle the word "Name" in sentence two.
4. Draw five small squares in the upper left-hand corner of this paper.
5. Put an X in each square.
6. Sign your name under the title of this paper.
7. After the title, write "Yes, yes, yes."
8. Put a circle around sentence seven.
9. Put an X in the lower left-hand corner of this paper.
10. Draw a triangle around the X you just put down.
11. On the back of this paper, multiply 703 by 66.
12. Draw a rectangle around the word "paper" in sentence four.
13. Loudly call out your first name when you get to this point in the test.
14. If you think you have followed directions carefully to this point, call out "I have."

15. On the reverse side of this paper, add 8950 and 9850.
16. Put a circle around your answer and put a square around the circle.
17. Count out in your normal speaking voice, from ten to one backward.
18. Punch three small holes in the top of this paper with your pencil.
19. If you are the first person to get this far, call out loudly, "I am the first person to this point, and I am the leader in following directions."
20. Underline all even numbers on the side of this page.
21. Put a square around every number written out on this test.
22. Say out loud, "I am nearly finished, I have followed directions."
23. Now that you have finished reading carefully, do only sentence two.

(Variations on this test show up from time to time on college campuses and military installations, where it is given to underscore the true meaning of following directions. This particular version appears in *Urban Folklore from the Paperwork Empire* by Alan Dundes and Carl R. Pagter, American Folklore Society, 1975.)

● **Thermodynamics of Political Gossip.** When affection for a sitting President cools down, the chatter about the senior available Kennedy heats up.

(*Newsweek,* May 8, 1978.)

● **Thidias's Law of Ironic Fate.** (Also known as, *Thyrsus's Law, Thyreus's Law, Thydeus's Law, Thidius's Law,* and *Agrippa's Law.*) When you go down in history, they'll spell your name wrong.

(N. Sally Hass, Sleepy Hollow, Ill.)

● **Thomas's Observation.** No child-proof bottle is absolutely "child-proof."

(John and Joyce Thomas, Grissom AFB, Ind.)

● **Thomas's Rules of the Game.** (1) No matter how well you do something, someone won't like it. (2) No matter how trivial the assignment, it is always possible to build it up to a major issue. (3) A good, illegible signature is a key to success.

(Robert H. Thomas, Farmington, Mich.)

● **Thompson's Publication Premise.** The probability of anyone reviewing a document in full diminishes with the number of pages.

(Charles I. Thompson III, Port Jefferson Station, N.Y.)

● **Thompson's Rule.** If you can't do anything about it, don't.

(William I. Thompson, West Hempstead, N.Y.)

● **Thurber's Amplification.** Love is blind, but desire just doesn't give a good goddam.

(James Thurber, in his *Further Fables for Our Time,* Simon and Schuster, 1966.)

● **Thurston's Law.** The higher the drifts, the harder to find a boy with a shovel.

("Thirsty" Thurston, in the *Hi and Lois* comic strip.)

● **Thwartz's Theorem of Low Profile.** Negative expectation thwarts realization, and self-congratulation guarantees disaster. (Or, simply put: if you think of it, it won't happen quite that way.)

(Michael Donner, editor of *Games* magazine, from the Editor's Message in the September/October 1979 issue. *DRW.*)

● **Tiberius's Law of Politicians.** Caesar doesn't want Caesar's. Caesar wants God's.
(N. Sally Hass, Sleepy Hollow, Ill.)

● **Tiller's Theory.** Car washing precipitates precipitation.
(George Tiller, Memphis, Tenn. Quoted in *Johns Hopkins Magazine,* May 1978.)

● **Tobias's Law.** The most sensible investments are mundane.
(Financial writer Andrew Tobias, who insists that it is easier, less risky, and a "better investment" to save $1,000 a year through special sales and discounts on everyday household items than it is to try to clear $1,000 in the stock market. Quoted in an interview in *The Baltimore Sun,* March 7, 1979. *ME.*)

● **Todd's Law.** In an area where the degree of confusion approaches infinite proportions—major disasters pass unnoticed.
(J. K. Todd, M.D., Calgary, Alberta.)

● **Tolkien's Reminder.** It does not do to leave a live dragon out of your calculations, if you live near him.
(J. R. R. Tolkien, quoted in *Reader's Digest,* September 1978.)

● **Tomlin's Request.** If love is the answer, could you rephrase the question?
(Lily Tomlin, quoted in *Time,* March 28, 1977.)

● **Toomey's Rule.** It is easy to make decisions on matters for which you have no responsibility.
(Jim Toomey, the St. Louis Cardinals, St. Louis, Mo.)

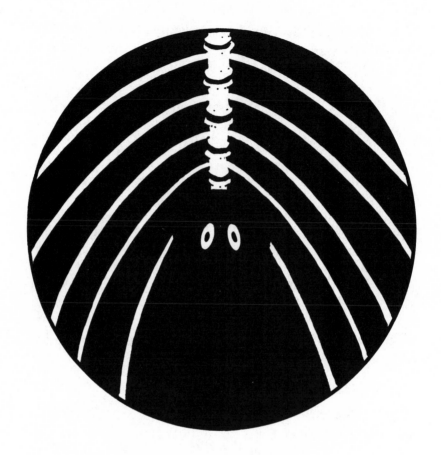

TOLKIEN'S REMINDER

- **Towson State College Rule.** If you are smart enough to fill out the application, you don't need to be here.
  (Towson State student/*Ra.*)

- **Trauring's Discovery.** Technical reports are expanded

from outlines, so that aides can recondense them for executive use.

>(Mitchell Trauring, Los Angeles.)

● **Treaty Ruling.** Treaties should be interpreted as to make sense, if possible.

>(U.S. Supreme Court. *TCA.*)

● **Tromberg's Laws.** (1) Oil is thicker than blood. (2) Just because you can do it doesn't mean you can make a living at it. (3) You ain't got it till you got it and even when you got it you may not. (4) When you see the word "net" in a contract, it means "nothing."

>(Sheldon Tromberg, writer/radio personality, Washington, D.C.)

● **Truman's Law of Qualifications.** Always vote for the better man. He is a Democrat. Anyone who votes for a Republican gets what he deserves.

>(Harry S Truman. *MBC.*)

● **Truman's Parental Instruction.** I have found that the best way to give advice to your children is to find out what they want, and then advise them to do it.

>(Harry S Truman. *MBC.*)

● **Tuchman's Axiom.** When something is perfect the way it is, someone will come along to improve it—and screw it up.

>(Stephan A. Tuchman, Rockville Center, N.Y., quoted in a letter to *Money* magazine on the magazine's new look. The letter appears in the February 1979 issue.)

● **Tufte's First Law of Political Economy.** The politicians who make economic policy operate under conditions of political competition.

(Edward R. Tufte, Professor of Political Science, Yale University, from his *Political Control of the Economy. TCA.*)

● **Turtle Principle, The.** If you go slow enough, long enough, you'll be in the lead again.

(Wayne Hoy, Rutgers University, Graduate School of Education. From Gerald Fava, Lake Hiawatha, N.J. Fava lists a few of the many areas in which the Turtle Principle applies:

Criminal Justice: victim's rights vs. criminal's rights.
Political Science: centralization vs. decentralization.
Physics: wave theory vs. particle theory of subatomic entities.)

● **Twain's Addendum.** Familiarity breeds contempt—and children.

(Mark Twain.)

● **Twenty-Third Qualm, The.**
The professor is my quizmaster, I shall not flunk.
He maketh me to enter the examination room;
He leadeth me to an alternative seat;
He restoreth my fears.
Yea, though I know not the answers to those questions, the class average comforts me.
I prepare my answers before me in the sight of my proctors.
I anoint my exam papers with figures.
My time runneth out.
Surely grades and examinations will follow all the days of my life,
And I will dwell in this class forever.
(U/TJR.)

● **Twyman's Law.** Any statistic that appears interesting is almost certainly a mistake.

(From Iwan Williams, London, who got it from A.S.C. Ehrneberg, Professor of Marketing, who got it from a colleague.)

● **Typesetter's Punctuation Rules.** Set type as long as you can hold your breath without getting blue in the face, then put in a comma. When you yawn, put in a semicolon. And when you want to sneeze, that's time for a paragraph.

(U/Ra.)

U

● **Udall's Fourth Law of Politics.** If you can find something everyone agrees on, it's wrong.

(Morris Udall, quoted in *The New York Times,* April 4, 1975.)

● **Umbrella Justice.**

> The rain it raineth on the just
> And also on the unjust fella;
> But chiefly on the just because
> The unjust stole the just's umbrella.

(Sir George Bowen, quoted by Senator William Proxmire, U.S. Senate, March 26, 1979.)

● **Unitas's Law.** If you hang around long enough, you'll end up somewhere.

(Quarterback Johnny Unitas, on being notified of his election to the Football Hall of Fame, January 29, 1979.)

● **United States Army Engineer General Orders.** (1) Measure it with a micrometer; mark it with a grease pencil; cut it with an ax. (2) If it doesn't fit, get a bigger hammer. (3) Pound to fit and paint to match.

(U.S. Army Engineer Training Brigade, Fort Leonard Wood, Mo. *MLS.*)

● **Universality of the So-Called "Rebel Yell."** Ain't nobody doesn't know to commence hollering "Yee-haw!" when circumstances dictate.

(U/RA.)

● **Upward-Mobility Rule.** Don't be irreplaceable. If you can't be replaced, you can't be promoted.
  (Desk sign/*Ra.*)

● **Useful Refrain.** When you're down and out, lift up your voice and shout, "I'M DOWN AND OUT!"
  (U/Ra.)

V

- **Van der Rohe's Explanation.** God is in the details.
  (Miës van der Rohe, from Anthony M. Cresswell, Evanston, Ill.)

- **Van Leuvan Storm Theory, The.** If it is raining now, and wasn't a little while ago, it is moving this way.
  (Jeff Van Leuvan, from his old college roommate, Earl Allen, Manhattan, Kans.)

- **Vargas's Varied Laws.** *Of Contrary Geography:* If the directions for finding a place include the words "you can't miss it," you will. *Of Free Booze:* People who hardly drink at all will imbibe stingers at 8:00 A.M. if the drinks are served on an airplane and free. *Of Paucity:* There is no such thing as a little garlic . . . or a mild heart attack . . . or a few children. *Of Jars:* A jar that cannot be opened through any combination of force, household tools, and determination will open instantly if picked up by the lid. *Of Human Statistics:* Figures don't lie, they lay.
  (Joie Vargas of Reno discovered all of these save for the last, which is from her husband, George L. Vargas.)

- **Vaughan's Rule of Corporate Life.** The less important you are on the table of organization, the more you'll be missed if you don't show up for work.
  (The late Bill Vaughan of *The Kansas City Star.*)

- **Vielmetti's Letter-into-Envelope Law.** If you think you have folded it enough, you haven't.
  (Ed Vielmetti, Michigan.)

● **Vietinghoff's Precept.** He who controls the forms controls the program.

(William F. Vietinghoff, Space Shuttle Main Engine Systems, Rockwell International, Canoga Park, Cal.)

● **Vogel's Rules.** (1) Nothing gives more satisfaction than telling a hypochondriac how well he is looking. (2) The length of a minute depends on which side of the bathroom door you're on. (3) The simplest incentive program: One mistake and you're through. (4) To shorten the winter, borrow some money due in the spring. (5) The wrong number on a telephone is never busy. (6) You will never lock your keys in the car at home.

(W. J. Vogel, Toppenish, Wash.)

W

● **Wain's Conclusion.** The only people making money these days are the ones who sell computer paper.

(U/DRW.)

● **Walker's Rule.** If you're there before it's over, you're on time.

(Politician James J. Walker.)

● **Wallace's Two-out-of-Three Theory.**
SPEED
QUALITY
PRICE
Pick any Two.

(James M. Wallace, Minneapolis. Wallace says that the dictum applies particularly to advertising, print shops, etc. He adds, "This is of course theoretical. In real life, one is usually hard-pressed to get any *one.*")

● **Warning-of-the-Century.** Do not place this Wine Brick in a one-gallon crock, add sugar and water, cover and let stand for seven days, or else an illegal alcoholic beverage will result.

(Label from a Prohibition-era product made of compressed grapes.)

● **Washington's First Law of Summer Survival.** Because so little of consequence happens here in August, whatever does occur is embellished, embroidered, and otherwise exaggerated far beyond reality.

(Political writer Robert Walters, who used the law to

explain *l'affaire* Andrew Young during the summer of 1979.)

● **Wattenberg's Law.** There is nothing so powerful as an old idea whose time has come again.
(Ben Wattenberg, quoted by Hugh Sidey in *The Washington Star,* May 6, 1979.)

● **Weiner's Wisdom.** Indecision is the key to flexibility.
(Lt. T. F. Weiner, USN, from R. J. Montore, Henderson, Ky.)

● **Weisert's Law.** If somebody will fund it, somebody will do it.
(Hilde Weisert, Teaneck, N.J.)

● **Welby's Law.** No problem is so deep or intractable that it can't be successfully overcome in the alloted time-slot.
(Named for TV's Dr. Marcus Welby. In a column by Alan M. Kriegsman in *The Washington Post,* January 19, 1979.)

● **Welch's Rule.** An apple every eight hours keeps three doctors away.
(David P. Welch, Bloomington, Ind.)

● **Wells's Law.** When in doubt, use clout.
(Stephen Wells, North Tarrytown, N.Y.)

● **Wemhoff's Law of Trade-offs.** Every advantage of any given course of action has a correspondingly equal and opposite disadvantage that, over the long run, fully offsets the advantage. *Corollary 1:* Over the short run, a specific advantage or disadvantage may predominate in any course of action. *Corollary 2:*

WEISERT'S LAW

Success in business consists in judging the short-run ascendancy of any specific advantage or disadvantage.
(Joseph A. Wemhoff, Chicago.)

● **West's Proven Facts.** (1) Man has yet to invent any substance that a Ping-Pong ball cannot get over, under, around, or through on its way to the most inaccessible spot in the playroom. (2) Electronically timed tests show that it takes a brand new tennis ball less than ten seconds to find, and stop dead-center in, the *only* puddle of water on any given tennis court. A ball that has been used until it barely bounces won't find such a puddle if you played all summer.
(Robert T. West, Minneapolis.)

● **Westheimer's Discovery.** A couple of months in the laboratory can frequently save a couple of hours in the library.
(Frank Westheimer, Harvard chemist, from Joseph A. Horton, M.D., Philadelphia.)

● **White House, First Law of Life in the.** Don't do anything you're not prepared to see in the papers the next morning.

> (Stated by a former White House staffer at the time of the Dr. Peter Bourne resignation. Quoted in *Newsweek,* July 31, 1978.)

● **White's Law.** Things are never as bad as they turn out to be.

> (Richard N. White, Director, School of Civil and Environmental Engineering, Cornell University.)

● **White's Observations of Committee Operation.** (1) People very rarely think in groups; they talk together, they exchange information, they adjudicate, they make compromises. But they do not think; they do not create. (2) A really new idea affronts current agreement. (3) A meeting cannot be productive unless certain premises are so shared that they do not need to be discussed, and the argument can be confined to areas of disagreement. But while this kind of consensus makes a group more effective in its legitimate functions, it does not make the group a creative vehicle—it would not be a new idea if it didn't—and the group, impelled as it is to agree, is instinctively hostile to that which is divisive.

> *(U/GT.)*

● **Whitehead's Injunction.** Seek simplicity—and distrust it.

> (Alfred North Whitehead to his students. From Sydney J. Harris.)

● **Whiteman's Findings.** *Wind Law for Pilots:* A head wind will reverse directions on the return flight. *First Corollary to Parkinson's Law:* Eight people will do ten people's work better than twelve people. *Measure of Success:* The measure of success is not how much money you have in the bank, but rather how much money the bank will lend you.

(Jack W. Whiteman, Phoenix.)

● **Whitney's Second Law of the Democratic Process.** In a democracy, having been born, death ensues. Everything else is negotiable.

(Peter Whitney, Tucson.)

● **Whole Picture Principle.** Research scientists are so wrapped up in their own narrow endeavors that they cannot possibly see the whole picture or anything, including their own research. *Corollary:* The Director of Research should know as little as possible about the specific subject of research he is administrating.

(U/DRW.)

WHY THIS BOOK WILL BRING YOU LUCK

Special Section 17

Why This Book Will Bring You Luck.

This book will bring you good luck. The luck is in your hands. Don't ruin it. You are to receive good luck within 14 days of buying this book if you follow instructions.

This is no joke.

To ensure your luck buy 20 additional copies and send them to people you think need good luck. Please do not send them money or any other book. All 20 books must be mailed within 96 hours.

Place the names and addresses of three of the 20 people at the bottom of this page along with your own name and address. Each subsequent recipient is to remove the top name when adding new names.

See what happens. It works. Accept no other chain letters. Dan G. of Denver has, at last count, 4,311 copies, and the estate of Harriet P. of Toledo has 1,406 copies (accumulated before she broke the chain and died).

Don't break the chain, and don't tell the spoilsport postal authorities about it.

● **Wickre's Law.** On a quiet night, there will always be two good movies on TV, or none at all.

(U/NDB.)

● **Wiio's Laws of Communications.** (1) Communication usually fails—except by chance. *Corollary:* If you are satisfied that your communication is bound to succeed, then the communication is bound to fail. (2) If a message can be understood in different ways, it will be understood in just the way that does the most harm. (3) There is always somebody who knows better than you what you meant by your message. (4) The more communication there is, the more difficult it is for communication to succeed. *Corollary:* The more communication there is, the more difficult it is for communication to succeed. *Corollary:* The more communication there is, the more misunderstanding will occur. (5) In mass communication it is not important how things are; the important thing is how things seem to be. (6) The importance of a news item is inversely correlated with the square of the distance.

(Professor Wiio, Director of the Institute for Communications Research at the University of Helsinki.)

● **Wilde's Maxim.** Nothing succeeds like excess.
(Oscar Wilde.)

● **Will's Paradox of Popular Government.** People are happiest when they are in a position to complain about government and they can complain with minimum confusion and maximum righteousness when they acknowledge, indeed insist, that government is not "by the people."

(Columnist George Will, in his *Washington Post* column for June 8, 1978.)

● **Williams's Critical Key.** Any critic can establish a wonderful batting average by just rejecting every new idea.

(J. D. Williams, quoted in Bennett Cerf's *The Sound of Laughter*, Doubleday, 1970.)

● **Williams's Law of Political Rhetoric.** Never underestimate the ability of a politician to (a) say something and tell you not very much, (b) do it with style, and (c) touch all the bases.
(Robert H. Williams, in *The Washington Post*. His proof was a statement made by Senator Henry M. "Scoop" Jackson to Israel's Prime Minister Menachem Begin: "As we Christians approach the Christmas season, we can all be thankful to a Moslem and a Jew.")

● **Willis's Law of Public Administration.** In any federal management report, the recommendations that would result in actual savings will be rejected, but the rejection will be "balanced" by the enthusiastic acceptance of those which increase costs.
(Bennett Moser Willis, McLean, Va., former Chief of Management, U.S. Department of Justice. He is also the author of the next item.)

● **Willis's Observation.** Except for courtship and travel, everything seems to take longer and cost more than: (a) it used to, (b) the estimate.

● **Willis's Rule of Golf.** You can't lose an old golf ball.
(John Willis, WCVB–TV, Boston.)

● **Wilson's Dietary Discovery.** It is impossible to lose weight lastingly and all diets are atrocious.
(Sloan Wilson, from *What Shall We Wear to This Party —The Man in the Gray Flannel Suit Twenty Years Before and After*, Arbor House, 1976.)

- **Winners' Law.** It isn't whether you win or lose, but how much you win by.

  (Paul J. Spreitzer, age fifteen, Chicago.)

- **Winston's Second Rule of Success.** Your greatest assets are other people's money and other people's patience.

  (Carl Winston, in *How to Run a Million into a Shoestring and Other Shortcuts to Success,* G. P. Putnam's Sons, 1960.)

- **Winter's Law of the Stranded.** The shortest distance to aid is in the opposite direction.

  (Robert F. Winter, M.D., Spring Valley, N.Y.)

- **Winters' Rule.** In a crowded place, the person directly behind you always has the loudest voice. *Corollary:* People with loud voices never have anything interesting to say.

  (Christine Winters, the *Chicago Tribune.*)

- **Woehlke's Law.** Nothing is done until nothing is done. (Richard A. Woehlke, Sutton, Mass. A few examples from the man who discovered the law: (1) Middle managers can never get the people they need for a job as long as they continue to muddle through by means of overtime, ulcers, and superhuman effort. But when enough people quit in frustration so that the job is not finished, upper management will approve the hiring of the necessary people. (2) Ditto for salaries. (3) The energy crisis [substitute your favorite crisis] will worsen until the whole house of cards collapses. Then and only then will effective measures be taken.)

- **Wohlford's Baseball Formula.** Ninety percent of this game is half mental.

(Outfielder Jim Wohlford, quoted in *Sports Illustrated,* October 24, 1977.)

● **Wolf's Law.** You never get a second chance to make a first impression.
(U/NDB.)

● **Wood's Incomplete Maxims.** (1) All's well that ends. (2) A penny saved is a penny. (3) Don't leave things unfinishe
(Donald R. Woods, Stanford, Cal.)

● **Woodruff's Work Rule.** *Everybody* works for the sales department.
(Jeff Woodruff, ABC. *MLS.*)

● **Woods's Rule for Drinking.** I always drink standing up because it is much easier to sit down when I get drunk standing up than it is to get standing up when I get drunk sitting down.
(Ralph L. Woods, from his book *How to Torture Your Mind,* Funk & Wagnalls, 1969.)

● **Woolsey-Swanson Rule of Problems.** People would rather live with a problem they cannot solve than accept a solution they cannot understand.
(Robert E. D. Woolsey and Huntington S. Swanson, from their book *Operations Research for Immediate Application: A Quick and Dirty Manual,* Harper & Row, 1975. *RS.*)

Y

● **Yoakum's Rule.** Don't put off until tomorrow what you can get done sometime next week.

(Robert Yoakum, Yoakum Features, Lakeville, Conn.)

● **Young's Law.** Nothing is illegal if one hundred businessmen decide to do it.

(Andrew Young.)

● **Young's Research Law.** All great discoveries are made by mistake. *Corollary:* The greater the funding, the longer it takes to make the mistakes.

(U/DRW.)

Source Code

AO. Alan Otten of *The Wall Street Journal.*
DRW. Donald R. Woods, Stanford, Cal.
EV. Elaine Viets, from her columns on laws in the *St. Louis Post-Dispatch.*
FSP. Frank S. Preston, Charlotte, N.C.
GT. Gregg Townsend, who is now in charge of the collection of laws that was begun by Conrad Schneiker and developed by Ed Logg and others. The seminal laws collection. Tucson.
JCG. Joseph C. Goulden, Washington, D.C.
JMcC. John McClaughry, Concord, Vt.
JS. John Shelton, Dallas.
JW. Jack Womeldorf, Washington, D.C.
MBC. Mark B. Cohen, Pennsylvania House of Representatives.
ME. M. Mack Earle, Baltimore.
MLS. Marshall L. Smith, Washington, D.C.
NDB. N. D. Butcher.
RA. Ryan Anthony, Tucson.
Ra. Radio. These are rules and laws that were called in to radio talk shows on which the author appeared to talk about the Murphy Center. Many of these are marked with *U* for unknown, as their authors typically did not have time or chance to give their full names.
RM. Robert Matz.
RS. Robert Specht, the RAND Corp.
TCA. Theodore C. Achilles, Washington, D.C.
TJR. Timothy J. Rolfe.
U. Unknown to the author.

Fellowships

As has been its custom since it was founded, the Murphy Center grants its coveted fellowships to those who have been of great help to its research effort. On rare occasion, Senior Fellows are appointed. These are people who have been of extraordinary help.

What follows is a listing of the new Senior Fellows and Fellows who have been added to the Center's official list since the publication of *The Official Rules*. To date more than five hundred names have been placed on the rolls of the Center. If nothing else, these distinguished people make us one of the most diverse institutions on the research landscape. In one period of a few days in late 1979, fellowships were granted to a ninth-grader, a rabbi, a Canadian priest, a nationally known columnist, a woman Air Force sergeant, a college student, a pilot, and a Pagosa Springs, Colorado, lady who wrote to the Center in praise of its first work with these kind words, "Once discovered, *The Official Rules* is like sex, indispensable." Not to brag too much, but the Center can now brag of enough M.D.'s to staff a good-sized hospital, enough Ph.D's to start its own university, and enough lawyers to tie up all the other Fellows for years.

245

Senior Fellows

Theodore C. Achilles

M. Mack Earle

Joseph C. Goulden

Frank S. Preston

Donald R. Woods

William L. Aamoth
Denis Abercrombie
Bob Ackley
Gustavo N. Agrait
Bernard L. Albert, M.D.
Marvin J. Albinak
Earl Allen
Wayne Allen
Ronald F. Amberger
Vic Anapolle
E. Frederick Anderson
Phil Anderson
Ryan Anthony
John C. Armor
Richard Arnold
Andrew G. Aronfy, M.D.
Michael Atkins
Juliet Awon-Uibopuu

Susan Baber
Penny Bair
Lawrence H. Ballweg
Ryan J. Barilleaux
Florenz Baron
Donald E. Bartel
H.A. Bartlett
Nick Becker
William J. Becker
Richard K. Beebe
Hal R. Belknap, M.D.
Norman R. Bell
Lennie Bemiss
William S. Bennett

James S. Benton
Martin Berger
Richard B. Bernstein
Thomas M. Beshere, Jr.
Richard N. Bialac
Wallace Bing
Sandra W. Bixby
Larry A. Blattenberger
Larry D. Bobbitt
A. S. Boccuti
Carl T. Bogus
Fred Bondy
Jonathan Bone
Warren Boroson
Ray Boston
David F. Brauer
Frank Brochu, M.D.
Robert N. Brodie
Ben Brodinsky
Arnold Brown
Dallas Brozik
E. H. Bulen
Henry B. Burdg
Bob Burkhart
N.D. Butcher
Richard Butler

William C. Callis
Constance E. Campbell
B. J. Carroll
Ron Carswell
Nelson Carter
Roger L. Cason

Clifton Chadwick
Stephen M. Chaplin
Vee Chilton
Milo M. Clarke
John S. Clayton
Leonard R. Cleavelin
Stephen Clifton
Nonnee Coan
Dianne Coates
Mark B. Cohen
Howard L. Cohodas
Kenneth B. Collins
M. C. "Chuck" Combs
Kevin Connor
Charles Conrad III
James E. Conrad
Ernest F. Cooke
Bruce C. Cooper
John H. Corcoran, Jr.
Clarence Cossey
Carson and Clive Court
Lloyd Craine
Les and Roxanne Cramer
William P. Creamer
Anthony M. Cresswell
Don Crinklaw
Ken Cruickshank
L.L. Cummings
Louise Curcio
Stewart Cureton, Jr.

Michael J. Daum
Donna P. H. Day
Alexander DeCicco
C. Henry Depew

Alfred deQuoy
Richard H. DeRoy
Thomas H. Dial
Isabelle C. Dickson
Larry G. Dowd

Tom Eddins
Robert V. Edwards
M. W. Egerton, Jr.
Edward L. Eisenstein
Owen Elliott
Robert W. Everett, Jr.

Dianne D. Farrar
Gerald M. Fava
Betty Feazel
Wayne C. Fields, Jr.
Richard Fitzmaurice
Joyce A. Flaherty
Sally Flanzer
Edward A. Flinn
T. Camille Flowers
John C. Foster
James F. Fox
Seth Frankel
Catherine B. Fresco
Steve Fried
Robert J. Friedman
B. A. Fuller
Randall Fullner

G. G. Gallagher
Jerome G. Ganci
David Gerrold
Robert D. Gillette, M.D.

Armando R. Gingras
Phil Ginsburg
Guy Godin
Gloria Gonzalez
Irwin Gooen
Robert Gordon
Frederick G. Gotwald
Paul Gray
John Greenyea
Mark Griesbach
Jean Sharon Griffith
Larry Groebe
Stephen J. Grollman
Gerald H. Grosso
John F. Gruber
John W. Gustafson

Meryl H. Haber, M.D.
T. L. Hakala
Keith W. Hall
Bob Hamm
Doug "Leo" Hanbury
Sally Handel
Mark D. Hanson
Sydney J. Harris
Annie C. Harvey
Andrew S. Hasselbring
W. Gilbert Hassett
Jane L. Hassler
Stanley H. Hayaski
John M. Hazlitt
David M. Hebertson
Curt Heinfelden
Mitch Hellman
Anita M. Herbst

Michael P. Herman
W. A. Herold
Pierre Allen Hill
Alan Hinds
Henry R. Hoffman, Jr.
Jon Hoffman
William G. Hogan
Alfred D. Holcombe
Howard R. Hollander
Clark Holloway
Stanley Horowitz
Joseph A. Horton, M.D.
John Hovancik
Hal Hoverland
Dwight A. Huster
Thomas L. Hutzler

Richard Isaac, M.D.

Andrew E. Jackson
Julie S. Jackson
Michael Jackson
Adrian Janes
Elizabeth W. Jefferson
Pat Jett
Rita Johnson
Kenneth J. Jones
D. Wylie Jordan, M.D.
Wally Juall
W. R. Jurgens

Shel and Susan Kagan
S. Karni
Connie Kass
Robert Katz

J. Jerry Kaufman
Donald Kaul
Gary E. Kautzmann
Joan C. Kaye
Barry Keating
Eleanor W. Keller
William S. Keller
David Kellough
Richard J. Keogh
Donald King
Larry King
Arthur E. Klauser
Robert P. Knowles
Gary Knowlton
Ron Koolman
Martin S. Kottmeyer
Gary R. Krafft

Stephen C. Lada
Robert V. Larson
Ed Laur
Rudy Lawton
Michael L. Lazare
Jack Lee
Lauren Leveut
Kenneth C. Levine
J. A. Lewandowski
Mike Lewis
Benjamin Lichtenberg
A. A. Lidberg
Fred Lightfoot
Wallace E. Lin
Ron Lindsey
Lewis P. Lipsitt
Jean Liston

Robert A. Liston
Lawrence Litt
E. A. Livingston
John Lockwood
Bob Loderstedt
Donald C. Loewe
Kevin G. Long
Dale Lowdermilk
Richard S. Luskin

Michael P. McCoy
Tom W. McLeod
Ian MacPherson
Carlisle Madson
Mike Manion
William F. Mann
Nancy Manske
Mark Manucy
Thomas Marguccio
P. W. Marriott
Wallace S. Marsh, M.D.
Maurice Marsolais
Robert Matz, M.D.
R. H. Mead
Liz Mendoza
Daniel J. Metzger
Robert Miazga
T. K. Mikadet
Don G. Miles
William Miles
Henry L. Miller
William M. Mills
Steven D. Mirsky
Kevin Mitchell
Norton Mockridge

Richard Molony
R. J. Montore
T. A. Moore III, M.D.
Terry C. Moore
Phil Moos, M.D.
Ronald J. Moran
John C. Morris, Jr.
Vivian M. Morrison
Pete Moutsatson
Georgette Muir
Ed Muldoon
Mariquita P. Mullan

Bert Nelson
Roger Newell
John T. Nolan
Ken S. Norris
Ronald M. Novinson
Andrew J. Novotney

Paul Obis, Jr.
Edward L. O'Brien
Vincent D. O'Connor
S. M. Oddo
Ted Olbrich
Clark Olmstead
Margaret K. Omar
Mike O'Neill
William O'Neill
David Ormerod
James B. Oshry
Jean Skinner Ostlund
Bill Ozard

Charles Pancoast

Joe Pangraze
Herbert H. Paper
Robert L. Pardieck
J. Thomas Parry
Denys Parsons
Carl M. Pearson
Layne B. Peiffer
John N. Petroff
Carol Pike
C. Kevin Price
Rose Primack

Martin Quigley
Alvin W. Quinn

J. Patricia Reilly
Robert E. Reynolds
Charles E. Rhodes
Edith K. Rice
Ken Rigsbee
Donald B. Rinsley, M.D.
Sarah Risher
Stephen P. Robbins
James A. Robertson
Michael A. Rogawski
Kenneth J. Rogers
Timothy J. Rolfe
Robert E. Rosa
Sal Rosa
Paul Rubin
George H. Rule
Gary Russell
Gene H. Russell

Patricia A. Samson

Robert J. Samuelson
Betty Sanders
Ellie Saraquese
Ken Schapiro
R. W. Scheussler
Eric M. Schlegel
Jerry Schonfeld
Warren K. Schoonmaker
Kenneth L. Schorr
Marc A. Schuckit
Paul Schulze III
Eldred O. Schwab
Warren Schwemer
Bill Scott
Sid Scott
Paul Seabury
Boake A. Sells
J. Richard Shanebrook
Stan Shannon
Virginia M. Sharples
Raymond J. Sheehan
John Shelton
Martin E. Shotzberger
K. W. Skinnell
L.J. Sklenar
Bob Skole
Larry M. Slavens
Don Smith
G. Guy Smith
Jerry Smith
John Stephen Smith
Ruth J. Smock
Richard C. Smolik
Barbara Solonche
Donald T. Spindel

Paul J. Spreitzer
Paul W. Steckel
Ashley H. Steele
Guy L. Steele, Jr.
Theodore Stern
James O. Stevenson
James V. Stewart
Richard Stone
J. M. Sullivan
John H. Sullivan
Joseph P. Sullivan
Larry W. Sussman
Robert A. Sweeney
Christopher Sybert
Mark Szymcik

David A. Tansik
Harri V. Taranto
Robert F. Tatman
Warren E. Taylor
John and Joyce Thomas
Robert H. Thomas
Charles I. Thompson
William I. Thompson III
Claude Timblin
August A. Toda
J. K. Todd, M.D.
Jim Toomey
Mitchell Trauring
Sheldon Tromberg

Joie and George Vargas
Ed Vielmetti
William F. Vietinghoff
Elaine Viets

W. J. Vogel
Ralph W. Voight

Michael J. Wagner
James M. Wallace
Robert Walters
Hilde Weisert
Andrew Weissman
David P. Welch
Stephen Wells
Joseph A. Wemhoff
Robert T. West
Richard N. White
Robert I. White, Jr., M.D.

Jack W. Whiteman
Peter Whitney
Iwan Williams
Bennett Moser Willis
John Willis
Ron Wilsie
Robert F. Winter, M.D.
Richard A. Woehlke
George Wolfford
Steven R. Woodbury

Robert Yoakum
William C. Young

The Murphy Center Newsletter

Volume 1. No. 1.

CENTER DENIED FOUNDATION GRANT WHICH IT DIDN'T ASK FOR IN THE FIRST PLACE: DIRECTOR HONORED

A letter from a top official of an important philanthropic foundation who was applying for a Center Fellowship ended his letter with the request that the Murphy Center *not* attempt to get a grant from his foundation. *"Our foundation,"* he explained, *"contributes only to frivolous programs, not serious ones like yours."*

The Director of the Center issued an immediate statement that said in part, "We think we are honored by this philanthropic first. As far as we can tell, we are the only research institute in the nation that not only does not have any foundation or government grants but has been peremptorily turned down for one. And for good reason."

Professor Puts Center Research to Good Use

A professor in the natural sciences, who shall remain nameless to protect his ruse, has found that the Center is a boon to his hobby of terrorizing graduate students. What this resourceful scientist does is to use oral examinations as a chance to ask hapless Ph.D candidates to recite and explain one or two of the

Center's laws, principles, or hypotheses. Invariably, the students conclude that the law in question is a key biological concept that they somehow missed during years of relentless study.

"Whatevers" Collection Growing

For reasons unclear, people have increasingly taken to sending the Center their pet "whatevers"—odds and ends that are hard to define save by example. Our file contains such gems as:

—A copy of the text that the late Rube Goldberg allegedly asked to have put on his tombstone: "Dear God, Enclosed please find Rube Goldberg. Now that you've got him, what are you going to do with him?"

—A sign found in a Japanese hotel room: "Please to bathe inside the tub."

—A yellowed clipping—undated, unsigned, unattributed—in which the writer suggests that there is deep satisfaction to be had from going out and intentionally violating conventional, proverbial wisdom. For instance, visiting a farm and putting all your eggs in one basket and then counting all your chickens before they're hatched.

—A small item from *The Wall Street Journal* reporting that Princeton University has installed a 3" × 5" card file-system to replace a computer that kept breaking down. (Two Fellows brought this to the attention of the Center.)

—More. Cartoons, religious tracts, "simple assembly instructions" that make no sense, chain letters, etc.

The Center is proud of this collection and thanks those who have helped start what may become one of the best whatever collections around.

New Research Suggested

From time to time, Fellows suggest new areas for Center investigation. Here is the best we have ever received:

> I might also mention that I have a very large collection of instances where persons' names and either their occupations or preoccupations are in synchrony. This is an area of human lawfulness which has not been sufficiently or seriously organized. I knew that there was orderliness here when I noted that on the Brown University campus a Mrs. Record was in charge of alumni files, Mr. Banks was the Controller, and Mr. Price was in charge of purchasing. Looking a bit beyond my own campus, I found that Dr. Fish was indeed the head of the University of Rhode Island Oceanographic Institute, and he had hired one staff member named Saila and another named Seaman. I won't belabor the situation further, beyond mentioning simply that my own research area is that of sucking behavior in infants.

Sincerely Yours,
Lewis P. Lipsitt
Professor of Psychology and Medical Science;
Director, Child Study Center.

Center Takes Up Arms . . . Motto

Resourceful friends of the Center have been most helpful in giving it a stronger institutional identity. Robert N. Brodie of New York City has suggested a slogan: "Ain't it the truth!" and Marshall L. Smith of Washington, D.C., has researched and presented us with the "Arms of the Edsel Murphy Family with Family Motto." The slogan, arms, and motto have all been officially adopted by the Center. Here are the arms with Smith's explanation.

ARMS OF THE EDSEL MURPHY FAMILY ADOPTED FOR
THE MURPHY CENTER
FOR THE CODIFICATION OF HUMAN AND
ORGANIZATIONAL LAW

Arms: Gules three mismatched cogwheels, *or* two monkey
wrenches salient, *or* three tack caltraps rampant.

Crest: An arm dressed, holding a broken pencil proper; spilt milk
and India ink mantling.

Motto: Calamitas Necessaria Es̄ (Disaster Is Inevitable).

Appendix

The Appendix has been removed.

Index

A

Absolute: Marguccio's; Shore's
Abstinence: Kaul's
Academia: Anderson's; Boroson's; Bressler's; Kerr's; Lowell's. *See also:* Education
Accidents: Bennett's
Achievement: Moore's; Ormerod's
Acquisition: Carlisle's
Action: Gomez's; Grizzly Pete's; Manske's; Moutsatson's; Obis's; Porter-Givens's; Ranger's; Rogers's; Thompson's
Adversity: Lipsitt's
Advertising: Field's; Leo's
Advice: Cureton's; Ganci's; Greenyea's; Juliet's; Masson's; Raper's
Age: Conrad's; Metzger's; O'Neill's; Sweeney's
Aid: Winter's
"Ain't": "Ain't"
Airplanes, Air Transportation/Aviation: Air Force Law; Lewandowski's; Reis's; Spaatz's. *See also:* Flying
Alcohol: Medical Principles; Warning
Ambidextrous: Greenhaus's
America: Dickson's; Great American Axiom
Anger: Jefferson
Animals: Morris's
Annual Reports: Henry's
Answers: O'Conner's
Apartment: Apartment dweller's; Highrise
Aphorism: Law
Apology: Parson's
Appearance: Business Maxims; Obvious
Apple: Welch's

Appliance, small: Smith's
Approval: Dmitri's
Arctic: Gould's; Peary's
Argot: How to:
Army: Civil Service; United States
Assembly: Christmas Eve
Assumption: Cason's; Tatman's
Astronomy: Olbers's
Atomic Attack: Emergency
Attendance: Berra's
Attitude: Business Maxims
Audition: Mirsky's
Auditors: Business Maxims
Authority: Jones's
Automobile/Automotive: Bennett's; Buxbaum's; DeCicco's; Dickson's; Hoffman's; Murray's; Vogel's
Average: Stephen's

B

Backfire: Quigley's
Balance of Payments: Callaghan's
Baldness: Daniels's
Balls: West's
Baseball: Custodiet's; Gomez's; Jackson's; Los Angeles; Raper's; Wohlford's
Bath: Dowd's
Bathroom: Campbell's
Beauty: Sally's
Behavior: Maslow's; Petroff's; Sweeney's
Behavior Modification: Gotwald's
Bicentennial: Explanations
Big Mac principle: Big Mac
Bills: Shelton's

C

Conscience: Conrad's
Conservative/Liberal: Conservative/Liberal; How to:
Constant: Leonard's
Consulting: Iron
Consumerism: Cruickshank's; Fullner's
Control: Vietinghoff's
Conviction: Giamatti; Quigley's
Cookies: Kaul's
Coolidge: Coolidge
Cooperation: Battista's
Corporations: Corporate; Vaughan's. *See also:* Organization
Correctives: Novotney's
Correlation: May's
Cost: Bryant's; Figley's; Guppy; Liston's (dictum); Miller's; Paulg's; Solis's; Willis's
Cost-effectiveness: Cost-effectiveness
Counting heads: Beebe's
Couples: Close's
Courage: Quigley's
Cows: Aquinas's
Crankiness: Henderson's
Creativity: Clay's; Johnson's
Credit: Business Maxims; Mockridge's
Crime: Kaul's
Critic: Williams's
Cuckoo Clocks: Daum
Cuneiform: Paper's
Curse words: Ranthony
Customers: Business Maxims

D

Dead end: Nelson's
Deadlines: Litt's
Death: Bradley's; Denenberg's; Kaul's; Maugham's; Miazga's
Debate: Knowles's
Deception: Obvious; Ozian
Decision/Decision-making: Arnold's; Bureaucratic; Fitzmaurice's; Hoadley's;

Iron; Kaplan's; Rangnekar's; Toomey's
Defense: Baron's; Dickson's (language)
Definitions: Science
Democracy: Greenfield's; Whitney's
Descriptions: Job performance
Design: Czusack's; Inch
Desk Jockey: Desk Jockey
Desperation: Hutzler's
Diagnoses: Medical principles
Diagrams: Official diagrams
Diet: Wilson's
Dining: Barilleaux's; Carlson's; Conner's; Dickson's; Howe's; Hubbard's; Marsolais's; Muir's; O'Brien's; Robertson's; Sans Souci; Solis's (Free Lunch)
Direction: Hildebrandt's; Holcombe's
Discards: Bell's
Disney World: Disney World
Disposal: Murray's
Distance: Healy's
Distinction: Miller's
Dog: Rover's
Do-it-yourself: Scott's
Dominance: Bronx
Doubt: Le Carré's, Wells's
Down and Out: Useful
Dragons: Bilbo's; Tolkien's
Drink: Allen's; Bacchanalian: Catch-22; Conrad's; Drunk: Slaven's; Vargas's; Woods's
Driving: Buxbaum's; Levine's; Stanley's
Drug: Medical principles
Dumb: Kraft's
Duty: Gracy's; McCabe's

E

Eagles: Allan's
Earaches: Medical principles
Earth-Water Kinesis: Kathleen's
Eating: Drogin's; Hartka's; Inge's; Momma's; O'Brien's; Sweeney's
Economics: Astor's; Berger's; Collins's;

F

G

H

I

J

K

L

M

Machines: Cooper's; Herman's
Mail: Arnofy's
Making ends meet: Quality
Male/Female: Field's; Fullner's; Parson's; Sally's
Man: Boorstin's; "Bugs" Baer's; Cuppy's; Eldridge's; Epperson's; Epstean's; Explanations; Field's; Hinds's; MIST (in the street); Montore's; Plato's; Quin's
Management: Ackley's; Rigsbee's
Manpower: Bone's
Maps: Jones's; Slim's
Marketing: Butler's
Marriage: Blattenberger's; Pietropinto's; Rosenblatt's
Martyrs: Howe's
Math: Jones's; Penner's
Maxims: Business
Measurement: Loderstedt's
Medes: Medes and Persians'
Media: Court's; Murray's
Medicine: How to; Medical principles; Welch's
Meetings: Cason's; Sklenar's
Memorandum: Memorandum; Oshry's; Rosa's
Memory: Hasselbring's; Hell's Angels' (novel)
Menus: Muir's
Metric: Explanations
Middle of the road: Loughrige's
Military: Herbst's; Krafft's; Slim's
Minutiae: Hassett's
Miseries: Miseries of 1806
Mistakes: Business Maxims
Money: Astor's; Barnum's; Berger's; Bryant's; Burns's; Business Maxims; Carolyn's; Dickson's; Disney World's; Dyer's; Figley's; Getty's; Glass's; Guppy's; Horomorun's; Hubbard's; Jefferson's; Johnson's; Kaul's; Meller's; Miller's; Money maxim; Notes; Owens's; Paulg's; Perlsweig's; Price's; Sieger's; Tromberg's; Wain's
Morality: Armor's
Moses: Bureaucratic survival
Motel: Dianne's
Mothers: Lee's; Mead's (in-law); Momma's; Nursing Mother's
Motivation: Spindel's
Motto: McLaren's
Mouse: Banacek's
Movies: Dowling's; Fonda's; Goldwynism; Wickre's
Mud-slinging: Adlai's
Murphylogical Research: Murphylogical
Murphy's Law: Boucher's; Metropolitan Edison's; Powell's; Short's;
Museum: Paper's
Music: Grant's; Leo's
Myth: Christmas Eve

N

Nature: Campbell's; Fowler's; Inge's
Necessity: Hall's
Necktie: Olsen's
Needs: Brecht's
Negativism: Kautzmann's; Nelson's
Negotiation: Laur's
Nerves: Griffith's
New England: Krutch's
News: Caffyn's; Powell's; Safire's;
Newspaper: Carter's; Slaven's
Nice Guys: Juall's
Nonsense: Corcoran's
North Dakota Null-Hypothesis Inventory, NDNI: Tests and Examinations
Notes: Peer's
Nothing: Jones's; Ranger's
Nuclear Attack: Bureaucracy and
Nursing Care: Carlisle's

O

Observation: Alfalfa's; Hall's; Harris's; MIST
Obsolescence: Hinds's
Official: Field's; Official Explanations
Oil: Energy matters; Q's; Tromberg's
Operation: Medical principles
Opinion: Cicero's
Optimism: Merrow's
Organization: Jacob's; Joe Cooch's; Jones's; Mary's; Organizational parable; Pearson's; Petroff's; Petronius Arbiter's; Rabinow's; Radovic's; Sheppard's; Sullivan's; Taylor's; Upward-Mobility; Vaughan's; Whitemen's; Woehlke's
Ornithological Statistic: Orben's
Outcome: White's Law
Output: Bartlett's
Overdoing: Bunuel's
Over the hill: Baker's
Owl: Banacek's
Oz: Ozian

P

Pain: Medical principles
Paper: Corry's
Paperwork: Lawrence's
Parable: Organizational
Paradox: Olbers's
Parenting: Forbes's; Mikadet's; Truman's
Parkinson's Law: Whiteman's
Parties: Burton's; Jinny's; Nelson's
Partners: Clarke's
Passport: Omar's
Patience: Bradley's; Raper's
Patients: Medical principles
Paucity: Vargas's
Payment: Gonzalez's
Pencils: Ma's; Napier's

Penny: Carolyn's
Pension: Civil Service
Pentagon: Sign
People: Business Maxims; Cloninger's; Heifetz's; Scheussler's
Performance: Newell's; Perfection
Periodical: Pancoast's
Permanence: Daugherty
Persians: Medes and
Personality: Blewett's; Masson's
Personal Worth: Gruber's
Pets: Hill's
Phenomenon: Fox's
Philadelphia: Rizzo's
Philanthropy: Philanthropy
Philosophy: Cicero's; Longworth's; Mills's; Santayana's; Sharples's
Phrase generator: How to:
Physics: Jackson's (food); Koolman's
Pigmentation: Russell's
Pigs: Business Maxims
Pilot: Pilot's
Pi R Rule: Pi R
Plagiarism: Clay's; Matthews-Butler
Planning: Pangraze's
Poison Ivy: Brauer's
Poker: Poker
Police: DeCicco's; Kaul's
Policy: Kaufman's
Politics: Abourezk's; Adams's; Baker's; Bendiner's; Cohen's; Congress; Coolidge's; Cotton's; DeRoy's; Disraeli's; Fannie's; Flak; Governor's; Landon's; Lippmann's; Miles's; Political (law); Political (leadership); Politico's; Rosenblatt's; Strout's; Thermodynamics; Tiberius's; Truman's; Tufte's; Udall's; Washington's; White House; Williams's
Polls: Rosalynn's
Poodle: Corcoran's
Popcorn: Corcoran's
Population: Taranto's
Possession: Midas's
Postal Service: Arnofy's; Gloom of Night
Potato Chips: Looney's

Q

R

Results: Nonreciprocal
Return: Hall's; Lincoln's
Reviews: Sissman's
Revolution: Khomeini; Novinson's
Right: Close's; Muir's
Roadblock: Kaufman's
Royalties: Otten's
Rubbernecking: Levine's
Ruination: Ruination
Rules: Bureaucratic Survival (Brownian); Mitchell's; Sit, Whittle, and Spit; Thomas's
Rumor: Agrait's; Buchwald's
Rush hour: Retsof's

S

Sacrifice: Patton's
Safety: Rizzo's
Saints: Notes
Sartorial Homogeneity: Sartorial
Satisfaction: Vogel's
Scandal: Strout's
Schools: Anderson's; Brogan's
Science: Le Bon's; Science; Notes; Shaw's
Scientist: Krupka's
Scissors: Aunt Emmie's
Score: Lansburgh's
Sea: Albert's; Erickson's
Seasickness: Cramer's
Seating: Bixby's
Second-chance: Wolf's
Second-sheet law: Morrison's
Seismological discovery: Russell's
Self-restraint: Augustine's
Seriousness: Modell's
Sermon: King's
Sex: Barrymore's; Corcoran's; Godin's; Horton's; Ruination; Seligson-Gerberg-Corman
Shavelson's Extension: Hellrung's
Shoes: Kathleen's

Shopping centers: Jackson's
Shrinkage: Corcoran's
Sibling: Family law
Silver lining: Spat's
Similarity: Lowell's
Simplicity: Craine's; Shannon's; Whitehead's
Sin: Korzybski's; Otten's; Remusat's
Singularity: Carson's
Sinking ship: Kaul's
Skylab: NASA
Smoke: Coccia's
Smoking: Aunt Emmie's; Joachim's
Snake: Reik's
Snow: Oshry's
Soap: Mykia's
Social Climbing: Cheshire's
Social investment: Fullner's
Society: Howe's; Nock's
Sociology: Cruickshank's; Meller's
Socks: Deborkowski's; Irreversible
Solution: Gordon's; Hellrung's; Human ecology; Jigsaw's; Stult's; Well's
Song: Leo's
Space: explanations
Speech: Adams's; Baker's; Coolidge's; Denenberg's; Faraday's; Hazlitt's; Olmstead's; Oxford
Sports: Ginsburg's; Lansburgh's
Square wheels: Arnold's
State service: State Service
Statistics: Bialac's; Callaghan's; Twyman's
Status: Crisp's
Storm: Van Leuvan
Strangers: Robert's
Strong mind: Slaven's
Structure: Matheson's
Style: Landers's
Suburban: Dickson's
Success: Alderson's; Bartel's; Borstelmann's; Business Maxims; Field's; Morford's; Peter's; Steckel's; Thomas's; Tromberg's; Whiteman's; Winston's
Suicide: Kaul's
Sum: Big Mac Principle
Supply and demand: Bethell's

LEARNING RESOURCES

CENTER

ILLINOIS CENTRAL COLLEGE
MCMLXVI

East Peoria, Illinois